Study Guide

to accompany

Gerow
ESSENTIALS OF PSYCHOLOGY

Study Guide

to accompany

Gerow
ESSENTIALS OF PSYCHOLOGY
Second Edition

Prepared by

Glenda Streetman Smith, PH.D.
North Harris College

HarperCollins*CollegePublishers*

Study Guide to accompany Gerow *ESSENTIALS OF PSYCHOLOGY, SECOND EDITION*

Copyright © 1996 HarperCollins*Publishers*

HarperCollins® and ▰® are registered trademarks of HarperCollins Publishers Inc.

All rights reserved. Printed in the United States of America. No part of this book may be used or reproduced in any manner whatsoever without written permission from the publisher. For information, address HarperCollins College Publishers, 10 East 53rd Street, New York, NY 10022. *For information about any HarperCollins title, product, or resource, please visit our World Wide Web site at **http://www.harpercollins.com/college***

ISBN: 0-673-99948-3

96 97 98 99 00 9 8 7 6 5 4 3 2 1

Table of Contents

PREFACE

You are beginning a wonderful adventure, an introductory psychology course. This study guide is designed to help you succeed. You will benefit most by familiarizing yourself with the design of the study guide and then working through each chapter as you read the corresponding chapter in your text.

Each chapter contains learning objectives, lessons on learning the vocabulary of psychology, practice tests in true-false, fill-in the blank, and multiple choice formats, and helpful study tips.

The learning objectives suggest what you should know when you have finished studying a chapter. However, don't limit your knowledge or interest to the objectives.

One of the most difficult tasks in an introductory psychology course is learning the considerable terminology. The sections titled **Vocabulary** are designed to help you with the new terms and definitions that you will encounter—not only in future psychology courses, but in many other courses and in many different contexts. The exercises are in a familiar matching format.

The practice tests consist of true-false, fill-in the blank, and multiple choice questions. Do not limit your studying to the information in these questions. They are intended to be just a sampling of the information in the chapter, not a comprehensive test. The answers to all the practice tests and the matching exercises are presented for all chapters at the end of the study guide.

Finally, **Essential Study Strategies** are ideas that my students have proven to be effective and efficient. I suggest that you read through these strategies in all fifteen chapters as soon as possible so that you may apply any or all of them right from the beginning of the course.

Use this study guide faithfully, and you will enjoy your successful adventure through psychology.

Study Guide

to accompany

Gerow
ESSENTIALS OF PSYCHOLOGY

CHAPTER 1—THE NATURE OF PSYCHOLOGY

LEARNING OBJECTIVES

The following items represent the fundamental concepts that you should know when you have finished studying this chapter. Read them now as a chapter preview and return to them to test your knowledge after you have studied.

Topic A
1. Define psychology?
2. List two points that must be demonstrated in order to claim that psychology is a science?
3. Explain how psychologists are scientist practioners.
4. Describe the subject matter of psychology and explain how operational definitions are used?
5. Discuss the ways that Descartes, Locke, Darwin, and von Helmholtz have influenced psychology?
6. Explain when and where psychology began and who should be credited with its origin?
7. Describe behaviorism and the psychoanalytic approach to psychology.
8. Describe the basic principles of humanism and gestalt psychology.
9. Describe the different areas of psychology and the sort of work a psychologist in each area would do.

Topic B
1. Define naturalistic observation and discuss the potential problems with its use.
2. Discuss how surveys and case history studies are used in psychology?
3. Explain why correlation is used, what data are needed to calculate a correlation coefficient, and the meaning of positive, negative, and zero correlation coefficients.
4. In the context of an experiment, define independent, dependent, and extraneous variables.
5. Explain how random assignment and baseline design contribute to control in experiments.
6. List the ethical guidelines in psychological research?
7. Discuss the importance of the interaction between nature and nurture?
8. Define phenomenology.
9. Discuss the claim that psychology is one of the most applied sciences.

VOCABULARY CHAPTER 1

On your own paper, write the definition for each of the following key terms. Your learning will be facilitated by writing the definition in your own words rather than copying the exact definition from your text.

PSYCHOLOGY

SCIENTIFIC METHODS

BEHAVIOR

AFFECT

INTERACTIVE DUALISM

STRUCTURALISM

BEHAVIORISM

HUMANISTIC PSYCHOLOGY

NATURALISTIC OBSERVATION

SURVEY

CASE HISTORY

CORRELATION COEFFICIENT

INDEPENDENT VARIABLES

EXTRANEOUS VARIABLES

CONTROL GROUP

BASELINE DESIGN

PHENOMENOLOGY

SCIENCE

HYPOTHESIS

COGNITIONS

OPERATIONAL DEFINITION

BRITISH EMPIRICISTS

FUNCTIONALISM

PSYCHOANALYSIS

GESTALT PSYCHOLOGY

OBSERVER BIAS

SAMPLE

CORRELATION

EXPERIMENT

DEPENDENT VARIABLES

EXPERIMENTAL GROUP

RANDOM ASSIGNMENT

DEBRIEF

MATCHING TOPIC 1A, B

Match the following key terms with the appropriate definition.

_____ 1. psychology		_____ 2. baseline design	
_____ 3. extraneous variable		_____ 4. case history	
_____ 5. scientific methods		_____ 6. science	
_____ 7. hypothesis		_____ 8. affect	
_____ 9. random assignment		_____ 10. operational definition	
_____11. interactive dualism		_____ 12. psychoanalysis	
_____13. British Empiricists		_____ 14. humanistic psychology	
_____15. behavior		_____ 16. Gestalt psychology	
_____17. functionalism		_____ 18. phenomenology	
_____19. behaviorism		_____ 20. structuralism	
_____21. independent variables		_____ 22. control group	

_____23. correlation coefficient   _____ 24. sample
_____25. debrief   _____ 26. naturalistic observation
_____27. cognitions   _____ 28. observer bias
_____29. survey   _____ 30. correlation
_____31. experiment   _____ 32. dependent variable
_____33. experimental group

a. Carefully and systematically watching behaviors of organisms as they occur naturally--without involvement of the observer.

b. The problem that occurs when the researcher's own motives, expectations, and past experiences interfere with the objectivity of observations.

c. The portion or subset of a larger population chosen for study.

d. An intensive, usually retrospective, and detailed study of some aspects of one (or a few) individual(s).

e. A number that indicates the nature (+ or -) and the strength (0.00 to +1.00 or -1.00) of the relationship between measured responses.

f. Events in an experiment that are manipulated by the experimenter that are hypothesized to produce changes in responses.

g. Factors in an experiment that need to be minimized or eliminated so as not to affect the relation between the independent and the dependent variable.

h. Participants in an experiment who do not receive any experimental treatment or manipulation.

i. The selection of members of a population in such a way that each has an equal opportunity to be assigned to any one group.

j. A method in which participants' performance with an experimental treatment is compared with performance without that treatment (the baseline).

k. To fully inform a subject about the intent and/or hypotheses of one's research once data have been collected.

l. Descartes' position that a separate body and mind influence each other and are thus knowable.

m. The scientific study of behavior and mental processes.

n. An approach to psychology emphasizing the person or self as a central matter of concern.

o. A means of collecting observations from a large number of subjects, usually by interview or questionnaire.

p. Mental processes involving one's feelings, mood, or emotional state.

q. A tentative explanation of a phenomenon that can be tested and then either accepted or rejected.

r. The study of events as they are experienced.

3

s. Philosophers (including Locke) who claimed, among other things, that the contents of the mind come from experience.

t. An approach to psychology that focuses on perception, particularly how we select and organize information from the environment.

u. An early approach to psychology emphasizing the scientific study of how the mind and consciousness help the organism adapt to the environment.

v. An approach associated with Freud, emphasizing instinctive strivings and an unconscious level of mind.

w. An approach to psychology emphasizing the overt, observable, measurable behavior of organisms.

x. A definition of a concept given in terms of the methods (or operations) used to measure or create that concept.

y. The school of psychology (associated with Wundt) interested in the elements and structure of the human mind.

z. A series of systematic approaches to problem solving, including observation, description, control, and replication.

aa. A statistical technique used to determine the nature and extent of the relationship between two measured responses.

bb. An organized body of knowledge gained through application of scientific methods.

cc. A series of operations used to investigate relationships between manipulated events (independent variables) and measured events (dependent variables), while other events (extraneous variables) are controlled or eliminated.

dd. The mental processes that include knowing, perceiving, thinking, and remembering.

ee. Participants in an experiment who receive a treatment or manipulation--there may be more than one in an experiment.

ff. Responses measured in an experiment whose values are hypothesized to depend upon manipulations of the independent variable.

gg. What an organism does: its actions, reactions, and responses.

TRUE-FALSE TEST TOPIC 1A

_____ 1. The ABCs of psychology are affect, behavior, and control.

_____ 2. Ruling out alternative explanations is a valid way of approaching a problem scientifically.

_____ 3. Most psychologists who are practitioners work in the business world.

_____ 4. Early philosophers are credited with focusing the study of human behavior away from the gods and more at the human level.

_____ 5. Though popular in the early years of psychology, both structuralism and behaviorism are virtually nonexistent in the current study of psychology.

_____ 6. Even though he was not a psychologist, Charles Darwin exerted great influence on the emerging field of psychology.

_____ 7. Early American teacher and writer William James thought of himself more as a philosopher than a psychologist.

_____ 8. Although her credentials were not formally recognized, Mary Calkins did significant research on human learning and memory.

_____ 9. John Watson is credited with changing the focus of psychology from the study of the mind to the study of behavior.

_____ 10. A real strength of Sigmund Freud was his research ability as a laboratory scientist.

_____ 11. Carl Rogers and Abraham Maslow founded the humanistic approach to psychology.

_____ 12. Behaviorism and Freud's psychoanalytic approach have in common their focus on the unconscious.

_____ 13. Gestalt psychology originated with a group of German scientists interested in perception.

_____ 14. The basic processes of the mind would be investigated by a cognitive psychologist.

_____ 15. Counseling psychologists and clinical psychologists have similar interests in helping individuals solve problems.

TRUE-FALSE TEST TOPIC 1B

_____ 1. One advantage of the case history method is that it can provide a wealth of information about a few individual cases.

_____ 2. A disadvantage of the case history method is that the information learned cannot be easily generalized to other cases.

_____ 3. Correlation coefficients range in value from negative one to positive one.

_____ 4. Correlation studies are widely used to demonstrate cause-effect relationships.

_____ 5. One advantage of the naturalistic observation method is its resistance to observer bias.

_____ 6. Control of extraneous variables is often easier with laboratory animals than with human subjects.

_____ 7. Most of what we know in psychology has been learned by conducting experiments.

_____ 8. The variable manipulated by the researcher is the independent variable.

_____ 9. Control in an experiment is often a matter of making sure that the control subject and the experimental subject begin the study on an equal basis.

_____ 10. In psychological research, safety is of great concern, but confidentiality does not really matter.

FILL-IN TEST TOPIC 1A

1. _____ is an organized body of knowledge gained by application of scientific methods.

2. A _____ is a tentative explanation of a phenomenon that can be tested and then supported or rejected.

3. Psychologists study affect, _____, and cognitions.

4. Descartes suggested that the mind and the body influence each other. This position became known as _____ _____.

5. _____ was a leader in the founding of the British empiricists, a group who credited experience and observation as the source of mental life.

6. _____ is a nineteenth century psychologist who made a significant contribution to the beginnings of psychology.

7. _____ was the founder of structuralism.

8. The approach to psychology favored by William James is known as _____.

9. _____ was the first woman to receive a Ph.D. in psychology.

10. _____ studied with William James, and although never awarded a Ph.D., made significant research contributions in the area of human learning and memory.

6

11. The psychologist who was responsible for psychology shifting from the study of the mind to the study of behavior was _____ _____.

12. _____ founded an approach that became known as psychoanalytic psychology.

13. The best meaning for the word "gestalt" is _____.

14. Carl Rogers is a well known contributor in the field of _____ psychology.

15. _____ psychology is the subfield that most directly seeks to identify those traits or characteristics that unite us as a species and at the same time can be used to differentiate among us.

FILL-IN TEST TOPIC 1B

1. Observer bias is particularly a problem in the _____ _____ research methodology.

2. A _____ is a subset or portion of a larger population that has been chosen for study.

3. An amnesia victim might be involved in a _____ _____ form of research.

4. The relationship between gas mileage and horsepower would likely be a _____ correlation.

5. Subjects who receive some treatment or manipulation are said to be members of the _____ group.

6. _____ _____ means that each research participant has an equal chance of being assigned to the control group or any of the experimental groups.

7. A research subject's name is usually not used in an experiment in order to provide _____ for the subject.

8. The _____ _____ _____ monitors ethical practices in psychological research.

9. _____ refers to our inherited characteristics, while _____ reflects the environmental influences that affect our development.

10. _____ is concerned with the study of events as they are experienced by the individual.

MULTIPLE CHOICE TEST TOPIC 1A

1. Psychology is the science of
   a. emotions and behavior.
   b. behavior and mental processes.
   c. cognitions and affect.
   d. human behavior.

2. To qualify as a science, a discipline must
   a. possess an organized body of knowledge and use scientific methodology.
   b. formulate hypotheses and test theories.
   c. be concerned with inanimate objects such as chemical reactions.
   d. be based on the thoughts and theories of great scientists.

3. A _____ is a tentative explanation of a phenomenon that can be tested and then supported or rejected.
   a. law
   b. theory
   c. scientific principle
   d. hypothesis

4. Interactive dualism was founded by
   a. Locke.
   b. Descartes.
   c. Darwin.
   d. von Helmholtz.

5. Margaret Floy Washburn is significant to the early history of American psychology because she
   a. founded functionalism.
   b. conducted significant experiments on human learning.
   c. was the first woman to earn a Ph.D. in psychology.
   d. encouraged the use of empirical methods.

6. Which of the following approaches in psychology would most likely be associated with this statement, "the whole is more than the sum of its parts?"
   a. humanism
   b. psychoanalysis
   c. gestalt
   d. structuralism

7. The city of Los Angeles has decided to make its offices "smoke-free" environments and wants a psychologist to teach smoking cessation classes for its employees. The type of psychologist most likely to do this job is a/an
   a. developmental psychologist
   b. educational psychologist
   c. clinical psychologist
   d. counseling psychologist

8. A couple having marital difficulties would most likely seek help from a/an
   a. health psychologist
   b. clinical psychologist
   c. counseling psychologist
   d. social psychologist

9. The subject matter of psychology is best described as
   a. perceptions, behavior, mental health.
   b. affect, behavior, cognition.
   c. thoughts, feelings, sensations.
   d. behavior, cognition, perception.

10. An office manager is interested in learning more about the characteristics of her coworkers, in order to build a spirit of team work and cooperation in the office. Which of the following psychology specialists would she most likely consult about this problem?
    a. personality psychologist
    b. clinical psychologist
    c. educational psychologist
    d. developmental psychologist

11. The psychological approach that suggests behavior is influenced by the unconscious is
    a. humanism.
    b. interactive dualism.
    c. phenomenology.
    d. psychoanalysis.

12. A significant contribution of the _____ approach was the emphasis
    placed on measurable observations.
    a. humanist
    b. gestalt
    c. psychoanalytic
    d. behaviorist

13. The humanistic approach to psychology was founded by
    a. Wundt and James
    b. Rogers and Maslow
    c. Watson and Skinner
    d. Freud and Jung

MULTIPLE CHOICE TEST TOPIC 1B

1. The work of Dianne Fossey, the researcher who studied gorillas in their own
   environment, is an example of
   a. experimentation
   b. correlation
   c. case history
   d. naturalistic observation

2. Observer bias is likely to present a problem in the _____ method of
   research.
   a. naturalistic observation
   b. case history
   c. experimental design
   d. correlation

3. The best research method for demonstrating a cause-effect relationship is
   a. experiment.
   b. survey.
   c. case history.
   d. correlation.

4. Surveys are the best research methods for
   a. demonstrating cause-effect relationships.
   b. controlling observer bias.
   c. gathering information about large numbers of people.
   d. assessing the nature of relationships between measures.

5. Correlation coefficients may range in value from _____ to ____
   a. 0 to 2
   b. -1 to +1
   c. 0 to +1
   d. -1 to 0

6. As a person's caloric intake increases, their weight gain also increases. This is an example of
   a. case history.
   b. naturalistic observation.
   c. negative correlation.
   d. positive correlation.

7. As study time increases, a student's tendency to make errors on a math exam decreases. This is an example of
   a. negative correlation.
   b. naturalistic observation.
   c. zero correlation.
   d. positive correlation.

8. The research method responsible for most of our knowledge in the field of psychology is
   a. experiment
   b. case history
   c. correlation
   d. survey

9. A researcher conducts a study in which he measures the visual development of kittens by their ability to negotiate a visual maze. Some of the kittens have been raised in normal light and some have been light deprived. In this experiment, the various light conditions would be the
   a. dependent variables.
   b. independent variables.
   c. extraneous variables.
   d. effect.

10. One advantage of using animals for research is that
    a. you don't have to worry with ethical considerations.
    b. they don't cost much.
    c. it is easy to control extraneous variables.
    d. baseline measures are easier with animals.

11. Techniques such as random assignment and baseline designs serve the common purpose of
    a. eliminating observer bias.
    b. maintaining ethical standards.
    c. controlling extraneous variables.
    d. making research subjects more comfortable.

12. Which of the following is/are ethical considerations for psychological research?
    a. The subjects' confidentiality must be guaranteed.
    b. Participation in research should be totally voluntary.
    c. Subjects must give advised consent.
    d. All of the above.

ESSENTIAL STRATEGIES FOR SUCCESS #1

DO'S AND DON'TS FOR EFFECTIVE TIME MANAGEMENT

Do: Study at a regularly scheduled time every day.
By studying everyday, you establish a good routine. This is important for two reasons. First, it helps get you started. As with other positive habits such as exercise, routine creates the attitude of expectation that you will do what has to be done. Second, research tells us that we learn more efficiently if we study for shorter sessions spaced over several days rather than cramming at the last minute.

Do: Know how much time you spend studying.
What other way is there to determine whether your study methods are effective and efficient? As a general rule of thumb, an average student should plan to spend two hours of study time for every hour of class. On a semester hour basis, most introductory psychology courses would consist of three hours of class per week. Therefore, MINIMUM study time should be at least six hours per week.

Do: Turn assignments in on time.
Always turn assignments in on time. It is senseless to turn an assignment in late and risk losing points when you are doing the work anyway. Do it on time.

Do: Review frequently.
Frequent reviewing is one of the keys to learning large amounts of complex information.

Do: Take short breaks every hour or so.
Studies indicate that the most efficient timing is to study for about fifty minutes to an hour and then take a short break of five or ten minutes. There are two exceptions to this: either writing a paper, or solving a complex problem in math or logic will benefit more from periods of continuous work (say two to three hours) without the interruptions of a break.

Do: Find time for fun.
Successful students find time for fun because they use efficient strategies that leave them time to do so and because they know the wisdom of the old adage, "All work and no play makes Jack a dull boy."

Don't: Study after 10 o'clock at night.
For most people, general alertness and mental efficiency decline late at night. Studies have shown that some students can accomplish in one hour earlier in the day what will take them an hour and a half to do later at night.

Don't: Procrastinate and try to get things done at the last minute.
Successful students enjoy getting assignments done and studying for exams ahead of time and then relaxing when they know they are fully prepared.

CHAPTER 2 —THE BIOLOGICAL BASES OF BEHAVIOR

LEARNING OBJECTIVES

The following items represent the fundamental concepts that you should know when you have finished studying this chapter. Read them now as a chapter preview and return to them to test your knowledge after you have studied.

Topic A
1. Describe the main structural features of the neuron, and the role of myelin.
2. Discuss the basic process involved when a neuron fires.
3. Explain how neural impulses are transmitted at the synapse.
4. Name four neurotransmitters and indicate some psychological reaction when each is involved.

Topic B
1. Explain how the nervous systems are structured.
2. Describe the major features of a spinal reflex and explain why spinal cord injury sometimes causes paralysis.
3. Discuss the medulla and the pons, their location and their functions.
4. Describe the cerebellum, its location, and its major function.
5. List the location and functions of the RAS, limbic system, hypothalamus, and thalamus.
6. Explain the location of the four lobes of the cerebral cortex and the sensory, motor, and association areas of the cerebrum.
7. Describe the split-brain procedure and differentiate the functions of the right and left hemispheres.

VOCABULARY CHAPTER 2

Write the definition for each of the following key terms. Your learning will be facilitated by writing the definition in your own words rather than copying the exact definition from your text.

NEURON	CELL BODY
DENDRITES	AXON
MYELIN	AXON TERMINALS
NEURAL IMPULSE	CHEMICAL IONS

RESTING POTENTIAL

NEURAL THRESHOLD

VESICLES

SYNAPTIC CLEFT

PERIPHERAL NERVOUS SYSTEM

AUTONOMIC NERVOUS SYSTEM

PARASYMPATHETIC DIVISION

MOTOR NEURONS

SENSORY NEURONS

SPINAL REFLEXES

MEDULLA

PONS

TREMORS

LIMBIC SYSTEM

THALAMUS

FRONTAL LOBES

MOTOR AREAS

CORPUS CALLOSUM

ACTION POTENTIAL

SYNAPSE

NEUROTRANSMITTERS

CENTRAL NERVOUS SYSTEM

SOMATIC NERVOUS SYSTEM

SYMPATHETIC DIVISION

ENDOCRINE SYSTEM

INTERNEURONS

SPINAL CORD

BRAIN STEM

CROSS-LATERALITY

CEREBELLUM

RETICULAR ACTIVATING SYSTEM

HYPOTHALAMUS

CEREBRAL CORTEX

SENSORY AREAS

ASSOCIATION AREAS

SPLIT-BRAIN PROCEDURE

MATCHING TOPIC 2A

Match the following key terms with the appropriate definition.

_____	1.	neuron	_____	2.	cell body
_____	3.	dendrites	_____	4.	axon
_____	5.	axon terminals	_____	6.	myelin
_____	7.	neural impulse	_____	8.	chemical ions
_____	9.	somatic nervous system	_____	10.	endocrine system
_____	11.	resting potential	_____	12.	synapse
_____	13.	vesicles	_____	14.	neurotransmitters
_____	15.	synaptic cleft			

a. The location where an impulse is relayed from one neuron to another by means of neurotransmitters.

b. Branchlike extensions from a neuron's cell body where most neural impulses are received.

c. A white fatty covering found on some axons that serves to insulate and protect them, while increasing the speed of impulses.

d. The difference in electrical charge between the inside of a neuron and the outside when it is at rest (typically about -70mV).

e. Complex chemical molecules released at the synapse which will, in general, either excite or inhibit neural impulse transmission.

f. A nerve cell, the basic building block of the nervous system, that transmits neural impulses.

g. The series of branching end points of an axon where one neuron communicates with the next in a series.

h. The small containers, concentrated in axon terminals, that hold molecules of neurotransmitter chemicals.

i. Electrically charged (either + or -) chemical particles.

j. A sudden and reversible change in the electrical charges within and outside the membrane of a neuron, which travels from the dendrite to the axon end of a neuron.

k. The space between the membrane of an axon terminal and the membrane of the next neuron in a sequence.

l. The short-lived burst of a change in the difference between the inside of a neuron and the outside of a neuron when it fires (typically about +40mV).

m. The long, tail-like extension of a neuron that carries an impulse away from cell body toward the synapse.

n. The minimum level of stimulation needed to get a neuron to fire.

o. The largest mass of a neuron, containing the cell's nucleus, which may receive neural impulses.

MATCHING TOPIC 2B

Match the following key terms with the appropriate definition.

_____ 1.	central nervous system	_____ 2.	peripheral nervous system
_____ 3.	somatic nervous system	_____ 4.	autonomic nervous system
_____ 5.	sympathetic division	_____ 6.	parasympathetic division
_____ 7.	endocrine system	_____ 8.	spinal cord
_____ 9.	sensory neurons	_____ 10.	motor neurons
_____ 11.	interneurons	_____ 12.	spinal reflexes
_____ 13.	brain stem	_____ 14.	medulla
_____ 15.	cross-laterality	_____ 16.	pons
_____ 17.	cerebellum	_____ 18.	tremors
_____ 19.	reticular activating system	_____ 20.	limbic system
_____ 21.	hypothalamus	_____ 22.	thalamus
_____ 23.	cerebral cortex	_____ 24.	sensory areas
_____ 25.	motor areas	_____ 26.	association areas

_____27. corpus callosum   _____ 28. split-brain procedure

a. The process of nerve fibers crossing over the brain stem so that the left side of the body sends impulses to and receives impulses from the right side of the brain, and vice versa.

b. The lowest part of the brain, just above the spinal cord, comprised of the medulla and the pons.

c. A network of glands that secrete hormones directly into the bloodstream.

d. A spherical structure at the lower rear of the brain involved in the smoothing and coordination of bodily movements.

e. The last sensory relay station; it sends impulses to the appropriate area of the cerebral cortex.

f. Those neurons of the ANS involved in the maintenance of states of calm and relaxation.

g. Those neurons in the brain and spinal cord.

h. Those areas of the frontal, parietal, and temporal lobes in which higher mental processing occurs.

i. A surgical technique of severing the corpus callosum, causing the two hemispheres to operate independently.

j. Those neurons of the ANS involved in states of emotionality.

k. Those neurons not found in the brain or spinal cord, but in the peripheral organs of the body.

l. Sensory and motor neurons outside the CNS that serve the sense receptors and the skeletal muscles.

m. The large, convoluted outer covering of the brain that is the seat of cognitive functioning and voluntary action.

n. A network of nerve fibers that interconnect the two hemispheres of the cerebrum.

o. Those neurons of the PNS that activate the smooth muscles and glands.

p. Automatic, involuntary responses that involve sensory neurons carrying impulses to the spinal cord, interneurons within the spinal cord, and motor neurons carrying impulses to muscles.

q. Neurons located within the spinal cord or brain.

r. A brain stem structure forming a bridge between the brain and the spinal cord.

s. Those areas of the cerebral cortex that receive impulses from our sense receptors.

t. A massive collection of nerve fibers within the spinal column that carry impulses to and from the brain and that are involved in some reflex actions.

u. Involuntary, trembling, jerky, movements.

v. Neurons that carry impulses toward the spinal cord or brain.

18

w. A small structure near the limbic system in the center of the brain, associated with feeding, drinking, temperature regulation, sex, and aggression.
x. Neurons that carry impulses away from the spinal cord or brain.
y. The strips at the back of the frontal lobes that control voluntary movement.
z. An area of the brain stem that monitors breathing and heart rate, and where most cross-laterality occurs.
aa. A network of nerve fibers extending from the brain stem to the cerebrum that is involved in maintaining levels of arousal.
bb. A collection of structures, including the amygdala and septum, which are involved in emotionality; and the hippocampus, involved in forming long-term memories.

TRUE-FALSE TEST TOPIC 2A

_____ 1. Myelin is the proper name for the gray matter of the brain.

_____ 2. The nucleus of a neuron is found within the cell body.

_____ 3. Dendrites receive messages from other neurons.

_____ 4. The neurons or nerve cells in the brain, although different from other cells in the nervous system, are essentially identical.

_____ 5. Myelin is most likely to be found on axons that carry impulses for long distances.

_____ 6. Myelinated fibers can carry neural impulses 10 times faster than unmyelinated ones.

_____ 7. Neural impulses are more comparable to a lightning storm than to fog.

_____ 8. The negative ions of a neuron are concentrated on the inside.

_____ 9. Neurotransmitters always excite the transmission of neural impulses.

_____ 10. Dopamine is a neurotransmitter associated with high levels of arousal.

_____ 11. Recent research with mice suggests that brain cells can be regenerated.

TRUE-FALSE TEST TOPIC 2B

_____ 1. The peripheral nervous system includes all the neurons found in the spinal cord and the brain.

_____ 2. Hormones are secreted into the bloodstream by the limbic system.

_____ 3. Many hormones and neurotransmitters are similar and can have similar effects.

_____ 4. The sympathetic and parasympathetic are divisions of the central nervous system.

_____ 5. The spinal cord receives impulses from the body on the sensory neurons.

_____ 6. The higher on the spinal cord that injury takes place, the greater portion of the body that will lose function.

_____ 7. It is impossible to experience even the simplest automatic behaviors without the conscious voluntary action of the brain.

_____ 8. Due to cross laterality, a stroke victim who has suffered damage to the left side of the brain is likely to suffer the results in terms of damage to the right side of the body.

_____ 9. The brain stem consists of the medulla and the reticular activating system.

_____ 10. The thalamus and hypothalamus perform the same essential function, just at different levels.

_____ 11. Voluntary activity originates in the motor area of the cerebral cortex.

_____ 12. Patients who have undergone split-brain surgery appear quite normal unless they are engaged in laboratory tests.

FILL-IN TEST TOPIC 2A

1. Axons end in _____ _____ where one neuron communicates with others.

2. Neural impulses are speeded up by the insulation of a fatty substance called _____.

3. A single nerve cell is called a _____.

4. _____ _____ are particles that carry a small electrical charge that is either positive or negative.

5. When a neuron is stimulated, it is able to fire through the release of tension referred to as _____ _____.

6. The _____ is the location where a neural impulse is relayed from one neuron to another.

7. Neurotransmitters are concentrated in small containers called _____.

8. The minimum level of stimulation required for a neuron to fire is called the
_____ _____.

9. _____ is a neurotransmitter associated with impairment of movement.

10. _____ are the natural pain suppressors in the brain.

FILL-IN TEST TOPIC 2B

1. The _____ _____ _____ is made up of all the nerves and nerve fibers in the brain and spinal cord.

2. _____ are secreted into the bloodstream by the endocrine system.

3. The _____ division of the autonomic nervous system is active when we are relaxed and quiet.

4. _____ _____ are simple automatic behaviors that occur without conscious, voluntary action of the brain.

5. If you prick your finger with a needle, the messages will be carried to the brain by way of the _____ nervous system.

6. When you ride a roller coaster and you feel your heart rate increase, you know that the _____ division of the ANS is active.

7. Sensory neurons and their impulses enter the spinal cord on _____ roots.

8. The knee jerk is an example of a _____ _____.

9. The medulla and the pons make up the _____ _____.

10. The fact that the left side of the body sends impulses to and receives messages from the right side of the brain is a function of _____ _____.

11. The _____ _____ _____ is associated with patterns of being alert or sleepy.

12. The _____ is the part of the limbic system involved in forming memories.

13. The three major areas of the brain that have been mapped are the sensory areas, the motor areas, and the _____ areas.

14. The surgical technique that separates the two hemispheres in the cerebral cortex, known as split-brain procedure, was first done in an attempt to alleviate the symptoms of _____.

21

MULTIPLE CHOICE TEST TOPIC 2A

1. The estimated number of neurons in the human brain is
   a. 100 million.
   b. 100 billion.
   c. 10 trillion.
   d. 100 trillion.

2. The largest mass of the neuron is the
   a. axon.
   b. nucleus.
   c. dendrite.
   d. cell body.

3. The function of the dendrites is
   a. receiving neural impulses.
   b. sending neural impulses.
   c. storing neural impulses.
   d. unknown.

4. Which of the following is a function of myelin?
   a. speeds the transmission of neural impulses
   b. aids the production of new neurons
   c. promotes the regeneration of damaged neurons
   d. acts as a protective covering for the nucleus of the neuron

5. Research by Reynolds and Weiss indicates that
   a. the largest number of neurons are present at birth.
   b. during childhood damaged neurons can regenerate.
   c. in adolescence development of myelin is complete.
   d. under the right circumstances, neurons and supporting cells can be regenerated in the brains of mice.

6. Neurotransmitters are contained in the
   a. vesicles.
   b. cell body.
   c. nucleus.
   d. axon terminals.

7. The role of neurotransmitters is to
   a. inhibit the firing of neurons.
   b. enhance the firing of neurons.
   c. have no effect on the firing of neurons.
   d. either enhance or inhibit the firing of neurons.

8. The minimum stimulation required to get a neuron to fire is called the
   a. action potential.
   b. resting potential.
   c. neural threshold.
   d. ion differential.

9. After a neural impulse, a neuron is ready to fire again after about
   a. a few minutes.
   b. several seconds.
   c. a few hundredths of a second.
   d. a few thousandths of a second.

10. Neurotransmitters are stored in the
   a. synapse.
   b. synaptic cleft.
   c. vesicles.
   d. cell body.

11. The neurotransmitter which influences normal memory function is/are
   a. dopamine.
   b. acetylcholine.
   c. norepinephrine.
   d. endorphins.

12. Endorphins are neurotransmitters which affect
   a. motor skills.
   b. level of pain.
   c. memory function.
   d. anxiety and arousal.

MULTIPLE CHOICE TEST TOPIC 2B

1. The skeletal muscles and sense organs are served primarily by the
   a. autonomic nervous system.
   b. somatic nervous system.
   c. central nervous system.
   d. peripheral nervous system.

2. The system primarily related to behavior in the areas of motivation and emotion is the
   a. endocrine system.
   b. central nervous system.
   c. somatic nervous system.
   d. peripheral nervous system.

3. The most complex of the nervous systems and the one most in control of our behavior and mental processes is the _____ nervous system.
   a. parasympathetic
   b. central
   c. somatic
   d. peripheral

4. Adrian is watching a horror movie and has become frightened. Her heart is pounding and she is breathing rapidly. Although she may not be aware of it, her body is producing extra adrenaline. All these changes are in response to the
   a. central nervous system.
   b. sympathetic nervous system.
   c. parasympathetic nervous system.
   d. endocrine system.

5. The _____ neurons carry impulses from the brain or spinal cord to the muscles and glands.
   a. sensory
   b. inter
   c. motor
   d. dorsal

6. Paralysis may be caused by damage to the
   a. sensory neurons.
   b. motor neurons.
   c. spinal cord.
   d. cerebrum.

7. Smooth muscle movements such as swinging a baseball bat are controlled by the
   a. cerebellum.
   b. pons.
   c. medulla.
   d. cerebrum.

8. Which of the following is monitored by the hypothalamus?
   a. anger
   b. waking up
   c. itching
   d. feeling thirsty

9. Which of the following is NOT one of the three major areas of the brain that have been mapped?
   a. sensory
   b. motor
   c. affect
   d. association

10. Knowledge of the two hemispheres of the cerebral cortex has increased tremendously because of
    a. split-brain surgery.
    b. animal research using CAT scans.
    c. case studies like that of Phineas Gage.
    d. the work of researchers like Broca.

11. For most right handed individuals a stroke would be most damaging if it occurs in the
    a. right hemisphere.
    b. left hemisphere.
    c. cerebellum.
    d. temporal lobes.

12. Reflexes like eye blinks are controlled by the
    a. spinal cord.
    b. medulla.
    c. pons.
    d. cerebrum.

13. The fibers connecting the two hemispheres form the
    a. cerebral cortex.
    b. cerebral connector.
    c. corpus callosum.
    d. synaptic cleft.

ESSENTIAL STRATEGIES FOR SUCCESS #2

DOS AND DON'TS FOR DEALING WITH DISTRACTIONS

Do: Study in the library or other quiet place.
The library not only has the advantage of being quiet, but it keeps you away from numerous other distractions such as phone calls, interacting with roommates, even seeing your personal effects that may start you daydreaming or thinking of other things.

Don't: Eat or chew gum while you study.
Eating or chewing gum while studying is distracting for two reasons. First, the rhythmical chewing creates a physiological interference. You are likely to begin to read in rhythm with the chewing. This reading rate is much slower than normal and interferes with your reading comprehension. Remember the old childhood trick of rubbing your stomach and patting your head at the same time. Each activity interferes with the other. Reading and chewing are related in much the same fashion. The second reason for not eating is that the taste and smell of the food may serve as a reminder of a previous experience and thus send you off into a daydream. You will find it much more difficult to concentrate. If you are truly hungry, both the dining experience and your studying will benefit if you just take a break and eat.

Don't: Watch TV or listen to the stereo while you study.
Many research studies have shown that groups not listening to stereo or television perform better on memory and learning tasks than those groups who do listen. Regardless of how well you are now doing, you could improve by turning off these distractions.

Don't: Daydream or lose concentration.
Losing concentration causes you to lose precious study time. If this is a problem for you, refer to Essential Strategies for Success on reading a textbook and the importance of generativity emphasized in strategy #1. In addition, you may want to try the pencil cure. Keep a pencil or pen in your hand as you read or study. After every page attempt to write a brief summary of what you have read. You may list only key words or phrases. If you can do this, you know you have been concentrating. If not, you have caught yourself quickly and have only one page to reread.

Don't: Think about other things you should be doing.
If interfering thoughts about realistic concerns do distract you while studying, the best solution is to write them down. You will then have the problem preserved so that you can take care of it at a later time. This way, you have no need to keep mulling the problem over while you try to concentrate on studies.

CHAPTER 3—HUMAN DEVELOPMENT

LEARNING OBJECTIVES

The following items represent the fundamental concepts that you should know when you have finished studying this chapter. Read them now as a chapter preview and return to them to test your knowledge after you have studied.

Topic A
1. List the three stages of prenatal development and discuss the important developmental events that occur during each stage.
2. Discuss the impact of diet, drugs, and stress on prenatal development.

Topic B
1. List the reflexes that neonates possess and discuss their importance.
2. Describe the basic sensory capacities of the neonate.
3. Define accommodation, assimilation, and schemas.
4. Describe the cognitive skills that develop during each of Piaget's stages.
5. Discuss the criticisms of Piaget's theory.
6. Explain Kohlberg's theory of moral development.
7. Discuss the influence of collectivist versus individualist cultures on moral development.
8. Describe Erikson's eight stages of development.
9. Discuss the importance of attachment.

Topic C
1. Describe the physical changes that accompany adolescence and the onset of puberty.
2. Describe the challenge of identity formation in adolescence.
3. Discuss drug use and abuse in adolescence.
4. Describe sexuality in adolescence and the associated problem of teenage pregnancy.
5. Describe the characteristic developments of early adulthood, including marriage and family and career choice.
6. Discuss the issues that are typically faced during middle adulthood.
7. Describe the elderly population in the United States and the problems associated with ageism.
8. Discuss Kubler-Ross's theory of death and dying.

VOCABULARY CHAPTER 3

On your own paper, write the definition for each of the following key terms. Your learning will be facilitated by writing the definition in your own words rather than just copying the exact definition from your text.

CONCEPTION	ZYGOTE
PRENATAL PERIOD	VIABILITY
FETAL ALCOHOL SYNDROME	CHILDHOOD
NEONATE	SCHEMA
ASSIMILATION	ACCOMMODATION
SENSORIMOTOR STAGE	PREOPERATIONAL STAGE
CONCRETE OPERATIONS STAGE	CONSERVATION
FORMAL OPERATIONS STAGE	COLLECTIVISM
INDIVIDUALISM	ADOLESCENCE
PUBERTY	MENARCHE
IDENTITY CRISIS	AGEISM

MATCHING TOPIC 3A, B, C

Match the following key terms with the appropriate definition.

_____ 1.	zygote	_____ 2.	neonate
_____ 3.	conception	_____ 4.	viability
_____ 5.	fetal alcohol syndrome	_____ 6.	concrete operations stage
_____ 7.	assimilation	_____ 8.	accommodation
_____ 9.	schema	_____ 10.	prenatal period
_____ 11.	individualism	_____ 12.	collectivism
_____ 13.	ageism	_____ 14.	preoperational stage
_____ 15.	menarche	_____ 16.	formal operations stage
_____ 17.	adolescence	_____ 18.	identity status
_____ 19.	puberty	_____ 20.	conservation
_____ 21.	sensorimotor	_____ 22.	childhood
_____ 23.	attachment		

a. The moment when the father's sperm cell unites with the mother's ovum to produce the zygote.

b. The period of development from conception to birth.

c. The one-cell product of the union of sperm and ovum at conception.

d. A cluster of symptoms (e.g., low birth weight, poor muscle tone, intellectual retardation), associated with a child born to a mother who was a heavy drinker of alcohol during pregnancy.

e. The period of human development between birth and puberty (the onset of adolescence).

f. In cross-cultural psychology, the tendency to set goals and make decisions based on a concern for one's self or the individual.

g. The ability to survive without interference or intervention.

h. The newborn, from birth to age of 2 weeks.

i. In Piaget's theory, a system of organized, general knowledge, stored in long-term memory, that guides the encoding and retrieval of information.

j. The developmental period begun at puberty and lasting through the teen years.

k. In cross-cultural psychology, the tendency to set goals and make decisions based on a concern for the group and the common good.

l. The stage of physical development at which one becomes capable of sexual reproduction.

m. A female's first menstrual period, often taken as a sure sign of the beginning of adolescence.

n. The struggle to define and integrate one's sense of self and what one's attitudes, beliefs, and values should be.

o. Discrimination or negative stereotypes about someone formed solely on the basis of age.

p. In Piaget's theory, from age 7 years to age 12 years, when concepts can be manipulated, but not in an abstract fashion.

q. In Piaget's theory, an appreciation that changing the physical properties of an object does not necessarily change its essence.

r. In Piaget's theory, ages older than 12 years, when one can generate and test abstract hypotheses, and think as an adult, where thinking follows rules.

s. The process of adding new material or information to an existing schema.

t. A strong two-way emotional bond, usually between a child and his or her parent or primary caregiver.

u. In Piaget's theory, the process of altering or revising an existing schema in the light of new information.

v. In Piaget's theory, from birth to age 2, when a child learns by sensing and doing.

w. In Piaget's theory, from age 2 to 6, when a child begins to develop symbolic representations, but cannot manipulate them; also characterized by egocentricity.

TRUE-FALSE TEST TOPIC 3A

_____ 1. A human zygote is formed when each parent contributes 23 pairs of chromosomes that unite during conception.

_____ 2. The zygote stage typically lasts from week 2 to week 8 of the prenatal period.

_____ 3. During the stage of the zygote, cell differentiation begins.

_____ 4. During the embryonic stage, the male or female genitals are formed.

_____ 5. The fetus is generally unaffected by the nutrition of the mother.

_____ 6. A nutritional deficiency may threaten the developing baby, but not the pregnant woman.

_____ 7. Although research clearly establishes the harmful effects of smoking on the smoker, there is no evidence that smoking affects a fetus.

_____ 8. Miraculously, babies born to mothers who abused psychoactive drugs during pregnancy are not likely to experience addiction themselves.

_____ 9. A pregnant woman under stress may be unknowingly depriving her baby of oxygen.

_____ 10. The focus on the father's contribution to the health of the fetus focuses on the quality of his sperm.

TRUE-FALSE TEST TOPIC 3B

_____ 1. Most of a neonate's behavior is reflexive.

_____ 2. In general, the development of motor skills in infancy is rapid and orderly.

_____ 3. To some degree, all human senses are functional at birth.

_____ 4. There are no significant sex differences with regard to motor development.

_____ 5. Research indicates that newborns can engage in simple learning through conditioning.

_____ 6. Robert Fantz demonstrated that babies prefer the sound of their own mother's voice.

_____ 7. Friedman demonstrated that babies between one and four days old have no memory capabilities.

_____ 8. Piaget's concepts of assimilation and accommodation refer to moral development.

_____ 9. Piaget's concept of schemas is observable in American and Swiss children, but not in children of other cultures.

_____ 10. Kohlberg proposed a stage theory of moral development.

_____ 11. Erikson's first stage of psychosocial development, trust vs. mistrust, occurs during late childhood.

_____ 12. About 65 percent of American children become securely attached by the age of one year.

TRUE-FALSE TEST TOPIC 3C

_____ 1. The biological definition for adolescence suggests that it begins with the onset of puberty and ends with the end of physical growth.

_____ 2. Over the past 25 years, the view of adolescence has changed from a picture of turmoil to a view of adjustments that are generally made in healthy ways.

_____ 3. Boys usually begin the growth spurt earlier than girls and end it with greater strength and size.

_____ 4. Biologically, puberty in males begins with the production of live sperm.

_____ 5. Whereas girls are very much aware of the onset of puberty, boys may not know when it occurs.

_____ 6. Kohlberg formulated the theory most related to identity crises.

_____ 7. Drug use declined in the 1980s and is continuing to decline in the 1990s.

_____ 8. Drug use among adolescents is greater than for any other segment of the population.

_____ 9. The largest increase in sexual activity is among males older than age 16.

_____ 10. Teenage pregnancy is less of a problem in the United States than in other developed countries.

_____ 11. The decision not to have children results in a decline in satisfaction later in life.

_____ 12. Middle-age spread is probably more of a reality than mid-life crisis.

_____ 13. The distinction between young-old and old-old is a valid one for psychologists.

_____ 14. The theory of Kubler-Ross that describes stages of grief in terminally ill patients is generally accepted without question or criticism.

FILL-IN TEST TOPIC 3A

1. The union of the _____ and egg cell is referred to as conception.
2. The stage of the _____ is the period during which the internal organs form.
3. A fetus has reached the point of _____ when it can survive and continue to develop after birth.
4. The stage of the _____ is the longest period of prenatal development.
5. The _____ _____ (disease) was significant to the discovery that the human fetus is not protected from the environmental agents experienced by the mother.
6. Symptoms of fetal alcohol syndrome include retarded physical growth, poor coordination, poor muscle tone, and _____ _____.
7. During pregnancy, when the mother experiences stress, the fetus may experience a reduced amount of _____.
8. Consuming _____ ounces or more of alcohol per day during pregnancy results in fetal alcohol syndrome.
9. About one third of the cases of _____ _____ are related to the quality of the father's sperm.
10. While concerns about how the mother's health and habits affect the baby focus on the pregnancy, concerns about influences from the father focus on _____.

FILL-IN TEST TOPIC 3B

1. During the first two weeks of life, the newborn is referred to as a _____.
2. Almost all behaviors of a newborn are _____.
3. Assessment of simple reflexive behaviors can be helpful in evaluating the _____ _____.

34

4. The apparatus used to test depth perception in children is called a _____ _____.

5. According to Piaget, a _____ is an organized mental representation of the world.

6. When children take new information and fit it into an existing schema, they are practicing _____.

7. When children change or revise existing schema, they are practicing _____.

8. When a child understands that changing the form or the appearance of something does not really change what the thing is, he/she has mastered _____.

9. _____ _____ is the final Piagetian stage of cognitive development.

10. Piaget has been criticized for his characterization of _____ in preoperational children.

11. _____ developed a stage theory of moral development.

12. Asian and South American cultures tend to be _____ as compared to the individualist orientation of the American culture.

13. _____ argued that Kohlberg misjudged sex differences in moral reasoning.

14. _____ _____ developed a theory of psychosocial development characterized by conflicts or crises to be resolved at each stage.

15. _____ is a strong, two-way emotional bond, usually referring to the relationship between a child and his or her mother or primary caregiver.

FILL-IN TEST TOPIC 3C

1. The view that adolescence is a period of turmoil, storm, and stress can be attributed to _____ _____ _____.

2. During adolescence, one of the most noticeable physical changes in boys is a change in their _____.

3. The onset of _____ marks a significant increase in the production of sex hormones.

4. _____ marks the onset of puberty in young girls.

5. The struggle to define and integrate a sense of who one is referred to as an
   _____ _____.

6. According to research by Shedler and Block, teenagers who were referred to as
   _____ in regard to drug use were better adjusted and psychologically
   healthier than the other groups studied.

7. During puberty, large doses of hormones stimulate the development of
   _____ _____ _____.

8. Girls in the United States younger than 15 are _____ times more likely to give
   birth than in any other developed country.

9. According to Erikson, the conflict to be resolved in early adulthood is intimacy
   versus _____.

10. One of the best predictors of successful marriage is the way the partners maintained
    _____ _____ before their marriage.

11. According to Turner and Helms, one is in the _____ stage of
    career development when one gives up part of the self to the job.

12. In the career stage of _____, the career decision is actually implemented.

13. According to Erikson, one who does not experience generativity in middle adulthood
    will experience _____.

14. Discrimination on the basis of age is referred to as _____.

15. The final stage of grief according to Kubler-Ross's theory is _____.

MULTIPLE CHOICE TEST TOPIC 3A

1. Growth is to enlargement as development is to
   a. maturation.
   b. differentiation.
   c. enhancement.
   d. maintenance.

2. During prenatal development, the baby is most sensitive to environmental influences
   during the
   a. first three months.
   b. second three months.
   c. third trimester.
   d. There is actually no difference, the fetus is equally sensitive throughout the
      pregnancy.

3. Which of the following is most likely to cause an increased risk of miscarriage or still birth?
   a. maternal stress
   b. maternal drinking
   c. maternal malnutrition
   d. maternal smoking

4. Which of the following drugs would a mother be safest in taking during pregnancy?
   a. penicillin
   b. tetracycline
   c. aspirin
   d. cocaine

5. A newborn is referred to as a
   a. fetus.
   b. embryo.
   c. neonate.
   d. baby.

6. The negative effect of maternal stress on the developing fetus is most likely related to the
   a. reduced flow of oxygen available to the fetus.
   b. increased metabolism in the mother, affecting the nutritional needs of the fetus.
   c. toxins produced by the mother's body as a reaction to the stress.
   d. father's failure to provide additional emotional support to the mother during pregnancy.

7. Which of the following abnormalities is most likely related to the father's condition at the time of conception?
   a. oxygen deprivation during prenatal development
   b. fetal alcohol syndrome
   c. Down's Syndrome
   d. discoloration of teeth and bones

8. Which of the following is NOT associated with smoking during pregnancy?
   a. mental retardation
   b. lower birth weight
   c. miscarriage
   d. visual defects

MULTIPLE CHOICE TEST TOPIC 3B

1. Which of the following is true of motor development?
   a. The sequence is orderly, but the rate is not.
   b. The rate is orderly but the sequence is not.
   c. Neither the rate nor the sequence is orderly.
   d. Both rate and sequence are irregular.

2. Which of the following is true of depth perception in infants?
   a. Psychologists have been unable to measure it precisely.
   b. By the time an infant can walk depth perception is developed.
   c. A baby in a cradle doesn't really need depth perception.
   d. By the time a baby can crawl depth perception is developed.

3. In order to assess memory in neonates, Friedman used
   a. the visual cliff.
   b. varying checkerboard patterns.
   c. pictures of the infant's mother.
   d. human faces.

4. Which of the Piagetian stages is marked by the development of conservation?
   a. sensorimotor
   b. preoperational
   c. concrete operations
   d. formal operations

5. Which of the following is NOT a criticism of Kohlberg's theory of moral development?
   a. It is more appropriate for individualistic cultures.
   b. The theory is sexually biased.
   c. Few people ever operate at the highest stages of moral reasoning.
   d. It is not valid in the cultures of Turkey, India, and Nigeria.

6. Hudson is considering taking a cookie even though his dad has told him not to. He thinks to himself, "I better not, because if I do, I'll be punished." This child is showing thinking characteristic of _____ morality.
   a. utilitarian
   b. preconventional
   c. conventional
   d. postconventional

7. A major strength of Erikson's theory is that it
   a. gives an opposing view of cognitive development.
   b. offers a better explanation of childhood cognitive processes.
   c. deals with social development instead of cognition.
   d. covers the entire lifespan, dealing with issues of adult development.

8. Which of the following is NOT a long-term benefit of secure attachment?
   a. higher self-esteem
   b. better relationships with siblings
   c. increased assertiveness
   d. greater attention spans

MULTIPLE CHOICE TEST TOPIC 3C

1. Anna Freud and G. Stanley Hall have in common their
   a. early training in psychoanalytic theory.
   b. belief that adolescence is a time of storm and turmoil.
   c. criticism of Kohlberg's theory of moral development.
   d. strict adherence to behaviorist principles.

2. Which of the following is NOT true of the growth spurt?
   a. Girls begin the growth spurt earlier than boys.
   b. Boys end the growth spurt with greater strength and size than girls.
   c. Increases in height and weight often occur so rapidly that they are accompanied by actual growing pains.
   d. The growth spurt affects all parts of the body uniformly.

3. The concept of the identity crisis faced by adolescents is part of the social development theory of
   a. Anna Freud.
   b. G. Stanley Hall.
   c. Lawrence Kohlberg.
   d. Erik Erikson.

4. According to a major study of adolescent drug use, the group who were better adjusted and more psychologically healthy were the
   a. abstainers.
   b. experimenters.
   c. frequent users.
   d. ones who could not be categorized.

5. Which of the following is NOT true of adolescent drug use?
   a. Over 45 percent of high school seniors report using illegal drugs.
   b. There are no differences in the rate of drug use between adolescents and adults.
   c. Drug use by secondary school students is declining in the 1990s.
   d. There are no racial differences in drug use.

6. Which of the following is NOT a negative effect of teenage pregnancy?
   a. The baby is at risk.
   b. Health care will be more costly for both mother and child.
   c. The mother is more likely to drop out of school.
   d. The mother is more likely to rely on welfare.

7. Choosing a marriage partner and deciding whether or not to have children may be related to Erikson's psychosocial stage of
   a. trust vs. mistrust.
   b. generativity vs. stagnation.
   c. intimacy vs. isolation.
   d. integrity vs. despair.

8. In terms of choosing marriage partners, which trait varies most cross-culturally?
   a. chastity
   b. mental ability
   c. socioeconomic status
   d. religion

9. Turner and Helms developed a theory suggesting that career choice involves seven stages. Which of the following stages involves the recognition that changes must be made to fit in with fellow workers and do the job as expected?
   a. reformation
   b. career clarification
   c. integration
   d. career clarification

10. If you have begun to face the challenge of dealing with other family members and now read the obituaries daily, you are probably in
    a. adolescence.
    b. middle adulthood.
    c. late adulthood.
    d. early adulthood.

11. In the stages of death and dying, the first stage is usually marked by
    a. denial.
    b. dealing with God.
    c. a sense of hopelessness.
    d. a rather quiet acceptance, facing the final reality of death.

ESSENTIAL STRATEGIES FOR SUCCESS #3

GETTING THE MOST FROM CLASS

Prepare for class by reading assignments ahead of time. As you read, make notes about topics that are particularly interesting to you. Also note any material you do not understand. Becoming familiar with the text information will invariably help you in taking notes as you will more readily understand the lecture material. You will not be struggling for spelling of key terms.

Pose potential questions that you can ask in class. Write them down. If there is something you don't understand, you can be sure there are others who are also finding the information puzzling. Asking questions is a good way to get involved and turn yourself on to a class that might otherwise be of less interest (although with the subject matter of psychology, I cannot imagine such a situation).

CHAPTER 4—SENSORY PROCESSES

LEARNING OBJECTIVES

The following items represent the fundamental concepts that you should know when you have finished studying this chapter. Read them now as a chapter preview and return to them to test your knowledge after you have studied.

Topic A
1. Define sensation, psychophysics, absolute threshold, difference threshold, and just noticeable difference.
2. Discuss signal detection theory.
3. Describe the processes of sensory adaptation and dark adaptation.

Topic B
1. Understand how the amplitude, length, and purity of light waves affect the psychological experience of light.
2. Discuss the major eye structures and their functions.
3. Discuss the rods and the cones and differentiate between the visual experiences attributed to each.
4. Compare and contrast the trichromatic and opponent-process theories.

Topic C
1. Discuss the three major physical characteristics of sound and the psychological experiences they produce.
2. Discuss the major structures of the ear and their functions.
3. Describe the stimulus, receptor, and primary qualities of the chemical senses.
4. Describe the cutaneous senses.
5. Explain the position senses and how they operate.
6. Explain how the sensation of pain is produced.

VOCABULARY CHAPTER 4

On your own paper, write the definition for each of the following key terms. Your learning will be facilitated by writing the definition in your own words rather than copying the exact definition from your text.

SENSATION   TRANSDUCER

PSYCHOPHYSICS   ABSOLUTE THRESHOLD
DIFFERENCE THRESHOLD   JUST NOTICEABLE DIFFERENCE
(JND)SIGNAL DETECTION THEORY   SENSORY ADAPTATION
DARK ADAPTATION   LIGHT
WAVE AMPLITUDE   BRIGHTNESS
WAVELENGTH   HUE
MONOCHROMATIC   SATURATION
WHITE LIGHT   CORNEA
PUPIL   IRIS
LENS   CILIARY MUSCLES
AQUEOUS HUMOR   VITREOUS HUMOR
RETINA   RODS
CONES   OPTIC NERVE
FOVEA   BLINDSPOT
LOUDNESS   DECIBEL SCALE
HERTZ   PITCH
TIMBRE   WHITE NOISE
PINNA   EARDRUM
MALLEUS, INCUS, STAPES   COCHLEA
BASILAR MEMBRANE   HAIR CELLS
TASTE BUDS   PHEROMONES
VESTIBULAR SENSE   KINESTHETIC SENSE

MATCHING TOPIC 4A

Match the following key terms with the appropriate definition.
_____ 1. sensation   _____ 2. transducer
_____ 3. psychophysics   _____ 4. absolute threshold
_____ 5. difference threshold   _____ 6. just noticeable difference
_____ 7. signal detection theory _____ 8. sensory adaptation
_____ 9. dark adaptation

   a. The process by which our eyes become more sensitive to light as we spend time in
      the dark.
   b. The study of the relationship between physical attributes of stimuli and the
      psychological experiences they produce.

c. The process of receiving information from the environment and changing that input into nervous system activity.

d. The minimal difference in some stimulus attribute, such as intensity that one can detect 50 percent of the time.

e. A mechanism that converts energy from one form to another as sense receptors do.

f. The view that stimulus detection is a matter of decision-making, of separating a signal from background noise.

g. The physical intensity of a stimulus that one can detect 50 percent of the time.

h. The smallest detectable change in some stimulus attribute, such as intensity.

i. The process in which our sensory experience tends (in most cases) to decrease or diminish with continued exposure to a stimulus.

MATCHING TOPIC 4B

Match the following key terms with the appropriate definition.

_____ 1. wavelength		_____ 2. light
_____ 3. iris		_____ 4. saturation
_____ 5. rods		_____ 6. pupil
_____ 7. brightness		_____ 8. white light
_____ 9. wave amplitude		_____ 10. lens
_____ 11. hue		_____ 12. retina
_____ 13. ciliary muscles		_____ 14. cones
_____ 15. blind spot		_____ 16. vitreous humor
_____ 17. aqueous humor		_____ 18. cornea
_____ 19. monochromatic		_____ 20. optic nerve
_____ 21. fovea		

a. A radiant energy that can be represented in wave form with wave lengths between 380 and 760 nanometers.

b. A characteristic of waveforms (the height of the wave) that indicates intensity.

c. The psychological experience associated with a light's intensity or wave amplitude.

d. A characteristic of wave forms that indicates the distance between any point on a wave and the corresponding point on the next cycle of the wave.

e. The psychological experience associated with a light's wavelength.

f. Literally one colored; a pure light made up of light waves all of the same wavelength.

g. The psychological experience associated with the purity of a light wave, where the most saturated lights are monochromatic and the least saturated are white light.

h. A light of the lowest possible saturation, containing a mixture of all visible wavelengths.

i. The outermost structure of the eye that protects the eye and begins to focus light waves.

j. The opening in the iris that changes size in relation to the amount of light available and emotional factors.

k. The colored structure of the eye that reflexively opens or constricts the pupils.

l. The structure behind the iris that changes shape to focus visual images in the eye.

m. Small muscles attached to the lens that control its shape and focusing capability.

n. Watery fluid found in the space between the cornea and the lens that nourishes the front of the eye.

o. The thick fluid behind the lens of the eye that helps keep the eyeball spherical.

p. Layers of cells at the back of the eye that contain the photosensitive rod and cone cells.

q. Photosensitive cells of the retina that are most active in low levels of illumination and do not respond differentially to different wavelengths of light.

r. Photosensitive cells of the retina that operate best at high levels of illumination and are responsible for color vision.

s. A fiber composed of many neurons that leaves the eye and carries impulses to the occipital lobe of the brain.

t. The region at the center of the retina, comprised solely of cones, with the best acuity in daylight.

u. A small region of the retina, containing no photoreceptors, where the optic nerve leaves the eye.

MATCHING TOPIC 4C

Match the following key terms with the appropriate definition.

_____ 1. hertz		_____ 2. malleus, incus, stapes
_____ 3. kinesthetic sense		_____ 4. taste buds
_____ 5. loudness		_____ 6. white noise
_____ 7. basilar membrane		_____ 8. pitch
_____ 9. pheromones		_____ 10. vestibular sense
_____ 11. decibel scale		_____ 12. pinna
_____ 13. timbre		_____ 14. cochlea
_____ 15. eardrum		_____ 16. hair cells

a. The psychological experience correlated with the intensity, or amplitude, of a sound wave.

b. A scale of our experience of loudness in which 0 represents the absolute threshold and 140 is sensed as pain.

c. The standard measure of sound wave frequency that is the number of wave cycles per second.

d. The psychological experience that corresponds to sound wave frequency and gives rise to high (treble) or low (bass) sounds.

e. The psychological experience related to wave purity by which we differentiate the sharpness, clearness, or quality of a tone.

f. A sound composed of a random assortment of all wave frequencies from the audible spectrum.

g. The outer ear that collects and funnels sound waves into the auditory canal toward the eardrum.

h. The outermost membrane of the ear that is set in motion by the vibrations of a sound; transmits vibrations to the ossicles.

i. (Collectively, ossicles) Three small bones that transmit and intensify sound vibrations from the eardrum to the oval window.

j. Part of the inner ear where sound waves become neural impulses.

k. A structure within the cochlea that vibrates and thus stimulates the hair cells of the inner ear.

l. The receptor cells for hearing, located in the cochlea, stimulated by the vibrating basilar membrane; they send neural impulses to the temporal lobe of the brain.

m. The receptors for taste located on the tongue.

n. Chemicals that produce an odor that is used as a method of communication between organisms.

o. The position sense that tells us about balance, where we are in relation to gravity, acceleration, or deceleration.

p. The position sense that tells us the position of different parts of our bodies and what our muscles and joints are doing.

TRUE-FALSE TEST TOPIC 4A

_____ 1. Sense receptors change physical energy into neural impulses through a process called sensation.

_____ 2. A light bulb and the receptors in your eye can both be thought of as transducers.

_____ 3. Transduction is the study of the relationships between the physical attributes of stimuli and the psychological experiences that they produce.

_____ 4. The techniques of psychophysics have given us the ability to test the sensitivity of our senses.

_____ 5. As threshold levels decrease, sensitivity levels increase.

_____ 6. The concept of absolute threshold is useful in testing the sensitivity of our senses.

_____ 7. Sensory thresholds are stable values that do not change over time.

_____ 8. Research subjects are more likely to say that they detect a sensory stimulus than to say that they don't.

_____ 9. Sensory adaptation is a slow process that takes place over a long period of time.

_____ 10. Sensory adaptation is facilitated by constancy of stimulation.

TRUE-FALSE TEST TOPIC 4B

_____ 1. The amplitude of a light wave is related to its intensity or brightness.

_____ 2. The wavelength of light is measured in nanometers.

_____ 3. The human eye is capable of detecting the full range of light waves.

_____ 4. The color of light is determined by its wavelength.

_____ 5. A monochromatic light is made up of waves that are all of the same amplitude.

_____ 6. Low saturation levels produce light that appears pale or washed out.

_____ 7. The colored part of the eye is the iris.

_____ 8. Two types of photoreceptors are the rods and the cones.

_____ 9. There is no vision in the blindspot because it lacks rods and cones.

_____ 10. Nocturnal animals see so well at night because their eyes have an abundance of cones.

_____ 11. The trichromatic theory of color vision suggests that there are three pairs of visual mechanisms that respond to different wavelengths of light.

_____ 12. Our best explanation of color vision is probably a combination of both the trichromatic theory and the opponent-process theory.

TRUE-FALSE TEST TOPIC 4C

_____ 1. The amplitude of a sound wave is related to its pitch.

_____ 2. The wave frequency of sound is measured in Hertz units.

_____ 3. Human ears are able to detect the full range of sound frequencies.

_____ 4. The psychological quality of a sound reflecting its purity is called timbre.

_____ 5. The hair cells in the ear have nothing to do with the hearing process.

_____ 6. Our sense of taste is referred to as olfaction.

_____ 7. A unique property of taste is that the receptor cells, the taste buds, can regenerate when they die.

_____ 8. All of the four basic taste qualities can be perceived on all areas of the tongue.

_____ 9. Pheromones carry sexually-related messages through the sense of smell.

_____ 10. The vestibular and kinesthetic senses are position senses.

_____ 11. Counterirritation is a process that can be used to ease pain.

_____ 12. Placebo effects apply in many other cases, but are not relevant to pain.

FILL-IN TEST TOPIC 4A

1. A _____ is a mechanism that converts physical energy in the environment into the neural energy of our nervous system.

2. The theory of _____ provides a means of relating the outside physical world to the inner psychological world.

3. _____ _____ theory attempts to explain the variation of sensory thresholds from moment to moment.

4. The smallest difference between stimulus attributes that can be detected is called _____ _____.

5. When _____ _____ occurs, our visual receptors actually become more sensitive to whatever small amount of light may be available.

6. Sense receptors respond best to _____.

FILL-IN TEST TOPIC 4B

1. The nanometer is the unit of measure for a wavelength of _____.
2. The properties of light are brightness, color, and _____.
3. Monochromatic light is highly _____.
4. Light that is the lowest possible saturation, containing a mixture of wavelengths is called _____ _____.
5. The pupil of the eye contracts in response to changes in levels of light or levels of _____.
6. The part of the eye where vision actually begins to take place is the _____.
7. Color vision relies heavily on the sight receptors called _____.
8. The primary colors for light are red, blue, and _____.
9. Negative afterimages provide support for the _____ theory of color vision.
10. _____ _____ proposed the opponent-process theory of color vision.

FILL-IN TEST TOPIC 4C

1. The loudness of a sound wave depends on the _____ of the wave.
2. The perceived loudness of a sound is indicated by its placement on the _____ scale.
3. A random mixture of sound frequencies produces _____ _____.
4. The pinna collects sound waves and sends them on to the _____.
5. The main structure of the inner ear is the _____.
6. Our senses of smell, texture, and temperature contribute heavily to our sense of _____.
7. The sense with the shortest, most direct pathway from the receptor site to the brain is the sense of _____.
8. Chemicals that produce distinctive odors are called _____.
9. The cutaneous senses include temperature and _____.
10. The _____ sense tells us about balance, where we are in relation to gravity.
11. A placebo is a substance that a person believes will be effective in treating a symptom such as _____.
12. _____ are the neurotransmitters that help reduce pain.

50

MULTIPLE CHOICE TEST TOPIC 4A

1. The conversion of energy from one form to another is
    a. sensation.
    b. adaptation.
    c. transduction.
    d. perception.

2. A researcher in psychophysics would be most likely to study
    a. perceptual decline in the elderly.
    b. cognitive aspects of perceptions.
    c. perceptual variables related to artistic ability.
    d. sensory thresholds in color-blind subjects.

3. Corey hears the so-called "silent" alarm that is present in many institutional buildings. Most people do not hear this high frequency pitch. It would be most accurate to say that in regard to hearing, Corey's absolute threshold is
    a. lower than that of most people.
    b. higher than that of most people.
    c. about the same except for certain frequencies.
    d. not functioning appropriately.

4. Beth works in a hospital. However, she is no longer aware of the offensive smell in the hospital. The best explanation for this is
    a. subliminal perception.
    b. signal detection theory.
    c. sensory adaptation.
    d. difference threshold.

5. The quality or characteristic of a stimulus that our sense receptors will most likely respond to is
    a. intensity.
    b. quality.
    c. change.
    d. constancy.

6. In order for a stimulus to be experienced, its intensity must be
    a. above absolute threshold.
    b. below absolute threshold.
    c. adapted by our senses.
    d. available in the environment.

7. Which of the following factors would not be considered important by signal detection theorists?
   a. background noise
   b. sensory adaptation
   c. level of attention
   d. subject bias

8. Which of the following stimulus factors would most likely lead to sensory adaptation?
   a. change
   b. intensity
   c. frequency
   d. constancy

9. Sue asks her husband, Bill if the blouse she has selected matches the new skirt she is buying. Sue is concerned with a/an
   a. absolute threshold.
   b. just noticeable difference.
   c. difference threshold.
   d. detected signal.

10. Applying the principles related to sensory adaptation, the best way to get attention from an audience to whom you are speaking is to
   a. speak louder.
   b. whisper.
   c. speak faster.
   d. all of the above.

MULTIPLE CHOICE TEST TOPIC 4B

1. Which of the following is NOT a characteristic of light waves related to our psychological experience of light?
   a. wave amplitude
   b. wavelength
   c. wave purity
   d. wave frequency

2. The color of a light is related to the _____ of the light wave.
   a. frequency
   b. length
   c. saturation
   d. amplitude

3. White light is produced by mixing
   a. wave lengths.
   b. wave amplitudes.
   c. rods and cones.
   d. monochromatic lights.

4. Monochromatic light is to white light as _____ is to _____.
   a. purity; impurity
   b. white; snow
   c. amplitude; wavelength
   d. saturation; timbre

5. The theory of color vision based on the idea that we possess three distinct receptor areas for the three primary colors of light is the
   a. primary color theory.
   b. signal detection theory.
   c. opponent process theory.
   d. trichromatic theory.

6. The fovea and the blindspot are both features of the
   a. cornea.
   b. lens.
   c. retina.
   d. pupil.

7. Which of the following statements is TRUE concerning the rods and cones?
   a. the rods outnumber the cones twenty to one
   b. they are represented in equal numbers in the eyes
   c. they function similarly
   d. they are found in different parts of the eye

8. There is no vision in the blindspot because
   a. the cornea is too curved to reflect light at that point.
   b. of disease in the cornea.
   c. there are no rods and cones there.
   d. the optic nerve is not connected there.

9. The part of the eye where vision is most acute is the
   a. fovea.
   b. iris.
   c. cornea.
   d. retina.

10. Sharon is trying to thread a needle, but the light is fairly dim. Due to the lack of light, the part of her eye that will help most in threading the needle is
    a. cones.
    b. rods.
    c. lens.
    d. cornea.

11. The phenomenon of negative afterimages lends support to the
    a. trichromatic color theory.
    b. opponent-process theory.
    c. existence of the blindspot.
    d. concept of color blindness.

12. People who are color blind most likely have a problem with their
    a. rods.
    b. fovea.
    c. iris.
    d. cones.

MULTIPLE CHOICE TEST TOPIC 4C

1. The amplitude of sound is measured in units called
   a. frequencies.
   b. Hertz.
   c. wavelengths.
   d. decibels.

2. Which of the following is NOT a correct match?
   a. sound intensity--wave amplitude
   b. timbre--wavelength
   c. pitch--wave frequency
   d. purity--wave frequency

3. A random mixture of sound frequencies produces
   a. white noise.
   b. sounds outside the range of human hearing.
   c. very intense sounds.
   d. sounds above 500 Hertz.

4. The actual receptor cells for hearing are contained in the
   a. pinna.
   b. eardrum.
   c. cochlea.
   d. stapes.

5. Pheromones carry messages that are related to
   a. sexual availability.
   b. sexual preference.
   c. repelling members of the opposite sex.
   d. identifying women with PMS.

6. Which of the following is NOT a correct match?
   a. taste--gustation
   b. smell--olfaction
   c. balance--vestibular sense
   d. cutaneous--kinesthetic

7. Motion sickness is the result of a disturbance of the _____ sense.
   a. kinesthetic
   b. vestibular
   c. visual
   d. cutaneous

8. The gate-control theory of pain proposes that pain actually occurs
   a. at the receptor cite.
   b. only in the external receptors.
   c. in the brain.
   d. only under intense stimulus levels.

55

9. Neurotransmitters that reduce the sense of pain are called
   a. enkaphalins.
   b. endorphins.
   c. pheromones.
   d. hormones.

10. Sharon's three-year-old son, Jess, is worried about going to the doctor to get a shot. To help him deal with the pain, Sharon should
   a. give him some apple juice and tell him it has magic power against pain.
   b. rub his arm vigorously near the area where he will get the injection.
   c. have him repeat the phrase, "It really won't hurt very much."
   d. all of the above.

ESSENTIAL STRATEGIES FOR SUCCESS #4

GETTING TO KNOW YOUR TEXTBOOK

1. Learn about the author.

Do this by reading the preface in the text. Check to see if there is a special note to students from the author. Also, look for any information about the author. Does the author specialize in a specific area of psychology? Is the author a faculty member at a college or university? Where? Where was the author educated? Has the author published other texts or scholarly writing?

2. Learn about the publisher.

What company published the text? Where is the company located? Have you used other texts by this publisher? What did you like or not like about them?

3. Learn about the book itself.

Read the table of contents to get an overview as to how the book is organized. Find out from your professor if the course organization will follow the structure of the book. Determine from your course calendar about how much of the text you will need to read on a weekly basis. What edition is the text? What does this mean? Look for the date of publication. How current is the text? Scan a few chapters. Look at the figures, tables, charts, graphs, cartoons, and any other illustrations. Note special features such as the running glossary, any appendices, and reference sections. How does the text read?

4. See Essential Strategies for Success #5

Look at the end of Chapter 5 for more information on reading your textbook.

CHAPTER 5—PERCEPTION AND CONSCIOUSNESS

LEARNING OBJECTIVES

The following items represent the fundamental concepts that you should know when you have finished studying this chapter. Read them now as a chapter preview and return to them to test your knowledge after you have studied.

Topic A
1. Define perception and consciousness.
2. Explain how and why stimulus factors influence perceptual selectivity.
3. Describe how personal factors are involved in perceptual selectivity.
4. Discuss the role of stimulus factors and personal factors in the organization of perceptual stimuli.
5. List the cues that help us perceive depth and distance.
6. Explain how the types of perceptual constancy operate.
7. Explain how illusions represent a failure of perceptual constancy.

Topic B
1. Define an altered state of consciousness and list William James' four basic characteristics of normal waking consciousness.
2. Discuss Freud's theory regarding levels of consciousness and the research that is bringing the unconscious into the laboratory.
3. Distinguish between the EEG and EMG.
4. Describe the four stages of sleep.
5. Explain how REM sleep differs from NREM sleep.
6. Define hypnosis, and describe how it affects consciousness.
7. Define dependence, tolerance, withdrawal, drug abuse, and addiction.
8. Discuss the effects of stimulant drugs, depressant drugs, hallucinogenic drugs, and marijuana.
9. Describe sleep disorders including insomnia, narcolepsy, and sleep apnea.

VOCABULARY CHAPTER 5

On your own paper, write the definition for each of the following key terms. Your learning will be facilitated by writing the definition in your own words rather than copying the exact definition from your text.

PERCEPTION   CONTRAST
MENTAL SET   GESTALT
FIGURE-GROUND RELATIONSHIP   PROXIMITY
SIMILARITY   CONTINUITY
COMMON FATE   CLOSURE
SUBJECTIVE CONTOURS   RETINAL DISPARITY
CONVERGENCE   ACCOMMODATION
PERCEPTUAL CONSTANCIES   ILLUSION
ELECTROENCEPHALOGRAPH   ELECTROMYOGRAPH
CONSCIOUSNESS   ALPHA ACTIVITY
REM SLEEP   ATONIA
HYPNOSIS   HALLUCINOGENS
PSYCHOACTIVE DRUG   DRUG ABUSE
STIMULANTS   DEPRESSANTS

MATCHING TOPIC 5A

Match the following key terms with the appropriate definition.

_____ 1. gestalt   _____ 2. figure-ground relationship
_____ 3. subjective contours   _____ 4. perceptual constancies
_____ 5. convergence   _____ 6. consciousness
_____ 7. perception   _____ 8. similarity
_____ 9. accommodation   _____ 10. illusion
_____ 11. common fate   _____ 12. closure
_____ 13. contrast   _____ 14. continuity
_____ 15. retinal disparity   _____ 16. mental set
_____ 17. proximity

a. The cognitive process of selecting, organizing, and interpreting those stimuli provided to us by our senses.

b. The extent to which a stimulus is in some physical way different from other surrounding stimuli.

c. A predisposed (set) way to perceive something; an expectation.

d. Whole, totality, configuration; where the whole is seen as more than the sum of its parts.

e. The Gestalt psychology principle that stimuli are selected and perceived as figures against a ground or background.

f. The Gestalt principle of organization that stimuli will be perceived as belonging together if they occur together in space or time.

g. The Gestalt principle of organization claiming that stimuli will be perceived together if they share some common characteristics.

h. The Gestalt principle of organization claiming that a stimulus or a movement will be perceived as continuing in the same direction or fashion as it started.

i. Stable patterns of perceiving the world that help us organize and interpret stimulus inputs.

j. The Gestalt principle of organization claiming that we tend to perceive incomplete figures as whole and complete.

k. The perception of a contour (a line or plane) that is not there, but is suggested by other aspects of a scene.

l. The phenomenon in which each retina receives a different (disparate) view of the same three-dimensional object.

m. The eyes moving toward each other as we focus on objects up close.

n. The process in which the shape of the lens is changed by the ciliary muscles.

o. A perception that is at odds with (different from) what we know as physical reality.

p. The awareness or perception of the environment and of one's own mental processes.

q. The Gestalt principle of organization in which we group together all the elements of a scene that move together in the same direction at the same speed.

MATCHING TOPIC 5B

Match the following key terms with the appropriate definition.

_____ 1. hallucinogens   _____ 2. depressants
_____ 3. hypnosis   _____ 4. electroencephalograph
_____ 5. psychoactive drug   _____ 6. REM sleep
_____ 7. electromyograph   _____ 8. drug abuse
_____ 9. alpha activity   _____ 10. stimulants
_____ 11. atonia

a. An instrument used to measure and record the overall electrical activity of the brain.

b. An instrument used to measure and record muscle tension/relaxation.

c. An EEG pattern associated with quiet relaxation and characterized by slow wave cycles of 8 to 12 per second.

d. Rapid eye movement sleep during which vivid dreaming occurs, as do heightened levels of physiological functioning.

e. Muscular immobility, associated with REM sleep, caused by the total relaxation of the muscles.

f. Drugs (such as alcohol, opiates, heroin, and barbiturates) that slow or reduce nervous system activity.

g. An altered state of consciousness characterized by an increase in suggestibility, attention, and imagination.

h. A chemical that has an effect on psychological processes and consciousness.

i. Drugs (such as LSD) whose major effect is the alteration of perceptual experience and mood.

j. A condition defined by lack of control, disruption of interpersonal relationships, difficulties at work, and a history of maladaptive drug use for at least one month.

k. Drugs (such as caffeine, cocaine, and amphetamines) that increase nervous system activity.

TRUE-FALSE TEST TOPIC 5A

_____ 1. Our perception is influenced by motivation, emotion, expectation, and experience.

_____ 2. We are more likely to attend to a stimulus if its intensity is different from the intensities of other stimuli.

_____ 3. Repetition is a stimulus factor that will draw attention to the stimulus.

_____ 4. Motivation, expectation, and intensity are personal factors that influence perceptual selectivity.

_____ 5. The concept of mental set applies to perceptual selectivity, but not to problem solving.

_____ 6. The behavioral psychologists had a special interest in perceptual organization.

_____ 7. Similarity, closure, continuity, and proximity are all examples of gestalt principles.

_____ 8. Cues for depth and distance involving both eyes are called binocular cues.

_____ 9. Convergence is a monocular depth cue.

_____ 10. When a woman looks in a small lipstick mirror, her lips will appear to be their normal size.

_____ 11. There are no cultural differences with respect to depth perception.

_____ 12. The effects of the Muller-Lyer illusion do not extend beyond the "carpentered world."

TRUE-FALSE TEST TOPIC 5B

_____ 1. William James suggested that there are three levels of consciousness.

_____ 2. According to Freud, aspects of one's experience that are not conscious but can easily be brought to consciousness are in the unconscious.

_____ 3. One problem with Freud's theory of consciousness is that it is difficult to test through controlled laboratory research.

_____ 4. An EEG measures brain activity, while an EMG measures muscle activity.

_____ 5. Dreams occur during REM sleep.

_____ 6. By stage three of sleep, the brain waves have changed from alpha to delta.

_____ 7. One explanation for why we don't remember more of our dreams is that they are just not interesting enough to motivate us to remember.

_____ 8. According to Freud, the reason for dreaming is to reveal our unconscious thoughts.

_____ 9. Everyone can be hypnotized.

_____ 10. Hypnosis produces such benefits as enhanced memory.

_____ 11. Both tolerance and withdrawal are associated with addiction.

_____ 12. Nicotine and caffeine are the most commonly used depressants.

_____ 13. Alcohol is the most deadly of all drugs.

_____ 14. A depressant is a drug that makes the user feel sadness.

FILL-IN TEST TOPIC 5A

1. Perception refers to the selection, organization, and _____ of stimuli.

2. _____ is the most common and important stimulus factor in determining attention.

3. _____ is a stimulus factor not related to contrast.

4. The _____ psychologists studied factors that influence perception.

5. The principle of _____ suggests that we tend to see things as ending up consistent with the way they started off.

6. Some cues about depth and distance require both eyes and are called binocular cues, while others known as _____ cues require only one eye.

7. When our perceptions seem to be at odds with what we know as reality, we are experiencing a/an _____.

8. _____ is a monocular depth cue.

9. Physical depth and distance cues come from the _____.

10. _____ _____ refers to our perception of objects maintaining their shape even though the retinal image they cast may change.

FILL-IN TEST TOPIC 5B

1. _____ developed the theory of levels of consciousness.

2. According to William James, consciousness is personal, continuous, changing, and _____.

3. Aspects of our experience that are the least known to us are stored in our _____.

4. A scientist interested in recording brain activity would use a/an _____.

5. When you have just closed your eyes, but are not yet asleep, your brain waves are called _____ _____.

6. _____ sleep is the period during which dreaming occurs.

7. _____ believed that dreaming provides the opportunity for fantasy and wish fulfillment.

8. During dreams, the muscles are inactive or immobilized. This is called _____.

9. _____ is the chronic inability to get to sleep and to get an adequate amount of sleep.

10. Hypnotized subjects are more open to _____.

11. Drugs that create changes in perception, mood, and behavior are referred to as _____ drugs.

12. A condition in which the use of a drug leads to a state where more and more of it is needed to produce the same effect is referred to as _____.

13. Dependence on drugs can be either physical or _____.

14. _____ is the most commonly used stimulant drug.
15. _____ are drugs that have the opposite effect of stimulants.

MULTIPLE CHOICE TEST TOPIC 5A

1. Boldface type in a textbook is an example of
   a. a stimulus factor in perception.
   b. a personal factor in perception.
   c. a stimulus factor in motivation.
   d. a gestalt principle of perception.

2. Which of the following is NOT a personal factor in perceptual selectivity?
   a. motivation
   b. past experience
   c. personality
   d. expectation

3. Which of the following stimulus factors are NOT contrast related?
   a. intensity
   b. size
   c. motion
   d. repetition

4. Psychological preparedness to perceive something in a given way is known as
   a. mental expectation.
   b. perceptual set.
   c. mental set.
   d. selective expectation.

5. Which of the following gestalt principles would most readily explain camouflage?
   a. similarity
   b. figure-ground
   c. continuity
   d. proximity

6. Events that occur close together in space or time are generally perceived as belonging together. Gestalt psychologists refer to this as
   a. proximity.
   b. closure.
   c. similarity.
   d. continuity.

7. Our perception of subjective contours is most related to the gestalt principle of
   a. proximity.
   b. common fate.
   c. similarity.
   d. closure.

8. We are able to experience 3-D movies because of the perceptual phenomenon of
   a. convergence.
   b. accommodation.
   c. similarity.
   d. retinal disparity.

9. Which of the following distance cues is limited to "arm's length?"
   a. convergence
   b. retinal disparity
   c. accommodation
   d. linear perspective

10. You are standing in the middle of a railroad track. As you look far ahead, the tracks seem to come together in the distance. This illustrates
    a. linear perspective.
    b. interposition.
    c. similarity.
    d. convergence.

11. Which of the following pictorial cues first came to the attention of Max Wertheimer during a train ride?
    a. relative size
    b. motion parallax
    c. patterns of shading
    d. texture gradient

12. You walk into a dark movie theater wearing a white shirt, and notice that the shirt now looks gray. However, you know that the shirt is still white because of
    a. size constancy.
    b. brightness constancy.
    c. linear perspective.
    d. texture gradient.

13. Which of the following is NOT an example of perceptual constancy?
    a. size
    b. shape
    c. color
    d. dimension

14. Most fish have monocular vision because their eyes are so far around on the sides of their heads. Which of these perceptual cues would be unavailable to a fish?
    a. size constancy
    b. accommodation
    c. convergence
    d. linear perspective

15. As Dorothy traveled down the "yellow brick road," if she looked down at her feet, the bricks would appear their normal size. However, if she looked ahead down the road, the bricks would appear to be smaller. This can be explained by the perceptual phenomenon of
    a. linear perspective.
    b. texture gradient.
    c. interposition.
    d. relative size.

MULTIPLE CHOICE TEST TOPIC 5B

1. Which of the following is NOT one of the characteristics attributed to consciousness by William James?
   a. stability
   b. personal
   c. continuous
   d. selective

2. Which of the following is NOT one of the levels of consciousness proposed by Freud?
   a. preconscious
   b. conscious
   c. unconscious
   d. post conscious

3. Which of the following statements concerning Freud's theory of levels of consciousness is TRUE?
   a. Contemporary research is attempting to demonstrate the existence of the unconscious as Freud described it.
   b. Most psychologists discount Freud's theory.
   c. Freud's theory has been acclaimed as lending itself well to experimentation.
   d. The levels of consciousness theory has some application in other areas, but not in the area of psychotherapy.

4. The major difference between an EEG and an EMG is that
   a. one measures brain waves and the other monitors heart rhythms.
   b. the EEG is less effective in monitoring altered states of consciousness.
   c. the EEG measures brain activity and the EMG measures muscle activity.
   d. one is used for accessing altered states brought about by sleep and the other for altered states brought about by drugs.

5. Which brain wave type is predominant in the first stage of sleep?
   a. sleep spindles
   b. alpha waves
   c. delta waves
   d. theta waves

6. In which of the sleep stages does dreaming occur?
   a. stage 1
   b. stage 2
   c. stage 3
   d. stage 4

7. Subjects deprived of REM sleep for a few nights and then left alone will spend long periods in REM sleep. This is referred to as
   a. microsleep.
   b. REM rebound.
   c. atonia.
   d. REM exaggeration.

8. Which of the following is NOT one of the accepted theories of the function of dreams?
   a. Dreaming allows for fantasy and wish fulfillment.
   b. REM sleep helps the brain consolidate memories of events that occurred during the day.
   c. Our dreams represent our deepest secrets and private fears.
   d. Dreams are the brain's interpretation of random activity.

9. Which of the following is NOT likely to occur during REM sleep?
   a. excitement of the sex organs
   b. elevated blood pressure
   c. marked decrease in physiological responses
   d. increased heart rate

10. Which of the following is NOT true of hypnosis?
    a. Avid readers and runners do not make good hypnotic subjects.
    b. People do not do anything under hypnosis that they would not do otherwise.
    c. Hypnosis can be used to alleviate pain.
    d. Hypnosis can not improve memory or learning ability.

11. The primary difference between drug dependence and drug addiction is
    a. dependence is psychological and addiction is physical.
    b. addiction is associated with tolerance and withdrawal, and dependence is not.
    c. dependence is associated with the less dangerous drugs.
    d. hallucinogens produce addiction, but not dependence.

12. The feeling of relaxation that smokers seem to enjoy can be attributed to
    a. the psychological effects of having something to do with their hands.
    b. the effect of nicotine on the brain.
    c. the ritual of smoking after meals and at other times when people are normally relaxed.
    d. the effects of nicotine on the central nervous system that causes muscle tone to relax.

13. Bennies, wakeups, and dexies are "street names" for
    a. hallucinogens.
    b. depressants.
    c. cocaine derivatives.
    d. amphetamines.

14. Being legally drunk is defined as having a blood alcohol level of
    a. 5 percent.
    b. 3 percent.
    c. 1 percent.
    d. 1/10 percent.

15. The most commonly used of all depressants is
    a. opiates.
    b. alcohol.
    c. barbiturates.
    d. heroin.

16. Which of the following drugs is most likely to produce hallucinations?
    a. heroin
    b. nicotine
    c. LSD
    d. alcohol

17. Which of the following is NOT associated with long-term marijuana use?
    a. bronchitis and other lung ailments
    b. chromosomal abnormalities in offspring
    c. hallucinations
    d. adverse effects on the immune system

18. The drugs which have the most unpredictable effect on consciousness are
    a. hallucinogens.
    b. barbiturates.
    c. stimulants.
    d. depressants.

ESSENTIAL STRATEGIES FOR SUCCESS #5

HOW TO READ YOUR TEXTBOOK

If you followed success strategy #4, you should be familiar with your text by now. In this segment, you will develop a system for chapter by chapter reading.

1. **Preread the chapter.**
   a. First read the outline at the beginning of the chapter. This will give you an idea as to its structure and organization. What topics are being covered? Are there issues with which you are already familiar?
   b. Then skip to the end of the chapter and read the summary. This will fill in a little more fully the ideas that will be presented in detail in the chapter. By reading this summary, you are preparing yourself to learn the more detailed information.
   c. Now skim through the chapter examining the charts, graphs, tables, figures, and any other illustrations. Students are tempted to ignore anything that isn't print. This is a big mistake. The author has carefully chosen these illustrations to emphasize and explain important points. See what you can learn from them. Think of them as sign posts indicating important material.
   d. Finally, read through the chapter taking only one section at a time. When you have finished a section, you need to check your comprehension in some way. Try to say out loud the major points or write them down. This is generativity that was mentioned in the first strategy for success. You must turn the passive process of reading into an active one.

2. **Plan to read the chapter only once.**
   For most people, rereading an entire chapter is a very inefficient study method. It is far better to do one thorough and comprehensive reading. In order to make this work, you must read actively.

3. **Keep a pencil and a highlighter handy.**
   Use the highlighter to underline important points that you want to return to or emphasize. Use the pencil to make notes to yourself in the form of questions or your own interpretations of what you have read. When you are ready to review, you should be able to review what you have underlined and the notes you have read. Reserve rereading only for the most difficult concepts or ideas which seem unfamiliar or unclear.

4. Sit at the keyboard.

I often use a strategy of sitting at a word processor and typing notes in the form of a summary or outline as I read. Then I study just my notes as I review, going back to the text only for clarification. Typing the notes is at least twice as fast as handwriting, even if you are a poor typist.

CHAPTER 6—LEARNING

LEARNING OBJECTIVES

The following items represent the fundamental concepts that you should know when you have finished studying this chapter. Read them now as a chapter preview and return to them to test your knowledge after you have studied.

Topic A
1. Define learning.
2. Describe the essential features of classical conditioning.
3. Define acquisition, extinction, spontaneous recovery, generalization and discrimination as they apply to classical conditioning.
4. Describe the sorts of responses that are most readily influenced by classical conditioning.
5. Describe the "Little Albert" experimental demonstration.
6. Understand what makes an effective CS.
7. Understand the importance of the time interval between the conditioned stimulus and the unconditioned stimulus.

Topic B
1. Explain the principles of operant conditioning.
2. Discuss shaping, acquisition, extinction, and spontaneous recovery in operant conditioning.
3. Understand the operational definition of reinforcer.
4. Distinguish between positive and negative reinforcement.
5. Give an example of a negative reinforcer and explain how negative reinforcement is used in escape and avoidance conditioning.
6. Distinguish between primary and secondary reinforcers.
7. Explain intermittent schedules of reinforcement and the advantages of using each of them.
8. Describe the effects and side effects of punishment.
9. Discuss discrimination and generalization in operant conditioning.

Topic C
1. Discuss the notions of cognitive maps and latent learning.
2. Relate the basic concepts of social learning theory and modeling.
3. Explain the role of vicarious reinforcement and vicarious punishment in learning.

CHAPTER 6 VOCABULARY

On your own paper, write the definition for each of the following key terms. Your learning will be facilitated by writing the definition in your own words rather than copying the exact definition from your text.

LEARNING
CLASSICAL CONDITIONING
UNCONDITIONED RESPONSE (UCR)
HABITUATION
CONDITIONED RESPONSE (CR)
EXTINCTION
GENERALIZATION
OPERANT
LAW OF EFFECT
EXTINCTION
SPONTANEOUS RECOVERY
REINFORCERS
NEGATIVE REINFORCER
SECONDARY REINFORCER
GENERALIZATION
LATENT LEARNING
SOCIAL LEARNING THEORY
VICARIOUS REINFORCEMENT (OR PUNISHMENT)
CONTINUOUS REINFORCEMENT SCHEDULE
INTERMITTENT REINFORCEMENT SCHEDULES

REFLEX
UNCONDITIONED STIMULUS (UCS)
ORIENTING REFLEX
CONDITIONED STIMULUS (CS)
ACQUISITION
SPONTANEOUS RECOVERY
DISCRIMINATION
OPERANT CONDITIONING
SHAPING
REINFORCEMENT
POSITIVE REINFORCER
PRIMARY REINFORCER
PUNISHMENT
DISCRIMINATION
COGNITIVE MAP

MATCHING TOPIC 6A

Match the following key terms with the appropriate definition.

_____ 1. acquisition
_____ 3. unconditioned stimulus
_____ 5. reflex
_____ 7. extinction
_____ 9. learning
_____ 11. classical conditioning
_____ 13. habituation

_____ 2. unconditioned response
_____ 4. conditioned stimulus
_____ 6. orienting reflex
_____ 8. discrimination
_____ 10. conditioned response
_____ 12. generalization
_____ 14. spontaneous recovery

a. Demonstration of a relatively permanent change in behavior that occurs as the result of practice or experience.
b. An unlearned, automatic response that occurs in the presence of specific stimuli.
c. Learning in which an originally neutral stimulus comes to elicit a new response after having been paired with a stimulus that reflexively elicits that same response.
d. In classical conditioning, a stimulus that reliably and reflexively evokes a response.
e. In classical conditioning, a response reliably and reflexively evoked by a stimulus.
f. The simple, unlearned response of orienting toward, or attending to, a new or unusual stimulus.
g. In classical conditioning, a simple form of learning in which an organism comes to ignore a stimulus of no consequence.
h. In classical conditioning, an originally neutral stimulus that, when paired with a UCS, comes to evoke a new response.
i. In classical conditioning, the learned response evoked by the CS after conditioning.
j. The process in classical conditioning in which the strength of the CR increases with repeated pairings of the CS and the UCS.
k. The process in classical conditioning in which the strength of the CR decreases with repeated presentations of the CS alone.
l. The phenomenon in classical conditioning in which a previously extinguished CR returns after a rest interval.
m. The phenomenon in operant conditioning in which a response that was reinforced in the presence of one stimulus appears in response to other similar stimuli.
n. The process in classical conditioning in which one CS is paired with the UCS and other stimuli are not.

MATCHING TOPICS 6B, C

Match the following key terms with the appropriate definition.

_____ 1. vicarious reinforcement   _____ 2. discrimination
_____ 3. negative reinforcer   _____ 4. latent learning
_____ 5. secondary reinforcer   _____ 6. cognitive map
_____ 7. extinction   _____ 8. positive reinforcer
_____ 9. spontaneous recovery   _____ 10. reinforcement
_____ 11. law of effect   _____ 12. reinforcers
_____ 13. social learning theory   _____ 14. shaping
_____ 15. intermittent reinforcement   _____ 16. continuous reinforcement
_____ 17. primary reinforcer   _____ 18. operant conditioning

_____19. generalization   _____ 20. acquisition
_____21. punishment

a. Increasing the rate (with reinforcement) or decreasing the rate (with punishment) of responses due to observing the consequences of someone else's behaviors.
b. The form of learning that involves changing the rate of a response on the basis of the consequences that result from that response.
c. The observation that responses that lead to satisfying states of affairs tend to be repeated, while those that do not, are not.
d. A procedure of reinforcing successive approximations of a desired response until that desired response is made.
e. The process in operant conditioning in which the rate of a reinforced response increases.
f. The process in operant conditioning in which the rate of a response decreases as reinforcers are withheld.
g. The phenomenon in operant conditioning in which a previously extinguished response returns after a rest interval.
h. A process that increases the rate or probability of the response that it follows.
i. Stimuli that increase the rate or probability of the responses they follow.
j. A stimulus that increases the rate of a response when that stimulus is presented after the response is made.
k. A stimulus that increases the rate of a response when that stimulus is removed after the response is made.
l. A stimulus (usually biologically or physiologically based) that increases the rate of a response with no previous experience required.
m. A stimulus that increases the rate of a response because of ITS having been associated with other reinforcers; also called conditioned, or learned, reinforcer.
n. A reinforcement schedule in which each and every appropriate response is followed by a reinforcer.
o. Reinforcement schedules in which appropriate responses are not reinforced every time they occur.
p. The administration of a punisher, which is a stimulus that decreases the rate or probability of a response that precedes it.
q. The process by which a response that was reinforced in the presence of one stimulus appears in response to similar stimuli.
r. The process of differential reinforcement in which one stimulus is reinforced while another stimulus is not.

s. Hidden learning that is not demonstrated in performance until that performance is reinforced.

t. A mental representation of the learning situation or physical environment.

u. The theory, associated with Bandura, that learning takes place through observation and imitation of others.

TRUE-FALSE TEST TOPIC 6A

_____ 1. Although learning is usually thought of as a good thing, it is clearly possible to learn bad habits as well as good ones.

_____ 2. Reflexes are learned through the process of habituation.

_____ 3. The term conditioned stimulus implies that some learning has taken place.

_____ 4. When a previously neutral stimulus begins to elicit a response, it has become a conditioned stimulus.

_____ 5. When a CS is repeatedly presented without being paired with the UCS, extinction will occur.

_____ 6. In classical conditioning, the CR and the UCR are actually different behaviors.

_____ 7. Discrimination training may be used to overcome the effects of generalization.

_____ 8. In classical conditioning, extinction is more like remembering than forgetting.

_____ 9. Conditioning is effective with behaviors, but not with emotions.

_____ 10. Recent research on classical conditioning indicates that any stimulus can become a conditioned stimulus.

TRUE-FALSE TEST TOPICS 6B, C

_____ 1. In operant conditioning, responses that produce positive consequences tend to increase and responses that produce negative consequences tend to decrease.

_____ 2. B.F. Skinner studied classical conditioning after Thorndike proposed the law of effect.

_____ 3. The law of effect suggests that responses are learned if they are preceded by the appropriate stimulus.

_____ 4. Operant conditioning usually does not result in the learning of a new response, but rather it results in a change in the rate of the response.

_____ 5. A negative reinforcer always increases the rate of the response it follows.

_____ 6. In cultures where the group is valued above the individual, reinforcing an individual's achievement will have less effect than in cultures that value individual effort.

_____ 7. Any stimulus can be a reinforcer once it is actually presented to the organism.

_____ 8. Positive reinforcement is effective in changing behaviors, but negative reinforcement is not.

_____ 9. Primary reinforcers are unlearned, whereas our desire for secondary reinforcers is learned or acquired.

_____ 10. Most of the reinforcers that humans work for are secondary reinforcers.

_____ 11. Continuous reinforcement schedules may actually reduce the effectiveness of a particular reinforcer.

_____ 12. To decrease the rate of the response, use negative reinforcement.

_____ 13. Fixed-interval reinforcement schedules produce responses that are easy to extinguish.

_____ 14. Learning that remains hidden until it is useful is called latent learning.

_____ 15. Bandura demonstrated that children can learn criminal behavior from adult live models.

FILL-IN TEST TOPIC 6A

1. _____ demonstrated the basic principles of classical conditioning.

2. A _____ is an unlearned, automatic response that occurs in the presence of a specific stimulus.

3. The stage of classical conditioning during which the strength of the conditioned response increases is called _____.

4. A stimulus that produces a response without any learning taking place is called a_____ stimulus.

5. In Pavlov's conditioning research, the conditioned stimulus was a _____.

6. When an extinguished response reappears automatically after a rest period, this is called _____ _____.

7. In classical conditioning, when a response is made to similar stimuli, we say that _____ has taken place.

8. The process in which an organism learns to make a conditioned response to only one conditioned stimulus, but not to other stimuli is called _____.

9. _____ is the psychologist who conducted the famous classical conditioning experiment with Little Albert.

10. _____ and Kamin are two researchers who study whether any stimulus can become a conditioned stimulus.

FILL-IN TEST TOPICS 6B, C

1. _____ developed the notion of the law of effect suggesting that responses are learned when they are followed by a "satisfying state of affairs."

2. Skinner is to _____ conditioning as Pavlov is to classical conditioning.

3. Skinner designed the operant chamber in order to control the _____.

4. _____ is an important influence on whether or not a person is motivated by individual rewards.

5. Rewarding successive approximations to elicit behavior is referred to as _____.

6. Stimuli that increase the rate of a response are known as _____.

7. _____ reinforcers do not require any previous learning in order to be effective.

8. The number of times a response is made when it is not being reinforced is referred to as _____ _____.

9. _____ is an example of a fixed-ratio reinforcement schedule.

10. A reinforcement schedule that does not reinforce every response is called a/an _____ reinforcement schedule.

11. _____ occurs when a stimulus delivered to an organism decreases the reate of probability of occurrence of the response that preceded it.

12. In order to be effective, punishment must be immediate and _____.

13. _____ learning involves the acquisition of knowledge or understanding.

14. _____ demonstrated that children learn aggression from models.

15. Learning about one's own behavior from watching the consequences of someone else's behavior is known as _____ reinforcement.

MULTIPLE CHOICE TEST TOPIC 6A

1. In classical conditioning, the relationship between the conditioned stimulus and the conditioned response is
   a. learned.
   b. reflexive.
   c. hereditary.
   d. conditioned.

2. When Pavlov repeatedly presented the conditioned stimulus without pairing it with the unconditioned stimulus, the conditioned response failed to occur. This is known as
   a. conditioning failure.
   b. recovery.
   c. extinction.
   d. habituation.

3. Nathan was in school when a tornado struck his community. Although no one was injured, he was terribly frightened. Now, he is afraid of all storms. This is an example of
   a. stimulus generalization.
   b. stimulus discrimination.
   c. spontaneous recovery.
   d. reflexive relationships.

4. John Watson's conditioning of Little Albert to fear a white rat was based on
   a. Little Albert's natural fear of the rat.
   b. the reflexive relationship between fear and loud noises.
   c. the child's natural anxiety in the presence of strangers.
   d. Little Albert's ability to generalize fear to many different stimuli.

5. You are writing furiously on an essay exam and all is quiet. Then someone enters the room and you stop and look up. You have displayed a/an
   a. conditioned response.
   b. generalized response.
   c. discriminatory reflex.
   d. orienting reflex.

6. Which of the following is the correct order of stimuli and responses during the acquisition stage?
   a. UCS-CS-CR
   b. UR-UCS-US
   c. CS-UCS-UCR
   d. CS-UCR-UCS

7. Spontaneous recovery of a classically conditioned response usually occurs immediately following
   a. the presentation of the UCS.
   b. acquisition.
   c. a rest period.
   d. extinction.

8. Research by Rescorla and Kamin recently demonstrated that
   a. rats do not experience food aversion.
   b. every stimulus cannot become a conditioned stimulus.
   c. lights will not become conditioned stimuli for rats.
   d. a tone will not serve as a UCS for fear responses in rats.

9. One problem with John Watson's research involving Little Albert is that
   a. the data were misinterpreted.
   b. Little Albert was an atypical subject.
   c. Watson and Rayner came to faulty conclusions.
   d. by today's standards, the research was unethical.

10. In classical conditioning, the first response made to the neutral stimulus is called a/an
    a. orienting reflex.
    b. learned response.
    c. reflexive response.
    d. unconditioned reflex.

MULTIPLE CHOICE TEST TOPICS 6B, C

1. Which of the following is NOT a correct pair?
   a. Watson and Rayner
   b. Skinner and Thorndike
   c. Pavlov and Bandura
   d. Rescorla and Kamin

2. Which of the following terms is LEAST common to both classical and operant conditioning?
   a. extinction
   b. stimulus generalization
   c. spontaneous recovery
   d. reinforcement

3. Positive reinforcement is to negative reinforcement as _____ is to _____.
   a. increase; decrease
   b. reinforce; punish
   c. apply; remove
   d. classical; operant

4. Primary reinforcer is to secondary reinforcer as _____ is to _____.
   a. breath; air
   b. unlearned; learned
   c. money; food
   d. intermittent; continuous

5. Which of the following is the best example of a primary reinforcer?
   a. food
   b. money
   c. paycheck
   d. new clothes

6. Claudia hit her head on the low ceiling in the playroom. After she rested for a while, the headache went away. It is likely that the resting behavior has now been
   a. positivelY reinforced.
   b. negatively reinforced.
   c. extinguished.
   d. punished.

7. Meredith receives a paycheck every Friday at noon, no matter how many hours she works that week. We might say that she is on a _____ reinforcement schedule.
   a. fixed ratio
   b. fixed interval
   c. variable interval
   d. variable ratio

8. Which of the following reinforcement schedules produces responses that are resistant to extinction?
   a. fixed ratio
   b. fixed interval
   c. variable ratio
   d. all of the above

9. Which of the following is NOT true of punishment?
   a. It is most effective if administered immediately.
   b. It should be administered consistently.
   c. It decreases only the punished response.
   d. It does not give the organism any information about appropriate behavior.

10. Which of the following could be attributed to Tolman's research?
    a. discovery of the law of effect
    b. the concept of cognitive maps
    c. the negative effects of punishment
    d. the role of classical conditioning in the formaiton of phobic disorders

11. A major implication of Albert Bandura's classic study with the BoBo doll is that
    a. children can and do learn all sorts of behaviors from watching television.
    b. children will do behaviors that they see others doing even when the others are punished.
    c. children will only do behaviors that are modeled by live models.
    d. children are most influenced by adult models viewed on television.

12. The learning that a college student does is best described by the _____ approach.
    a. cognitive
    b. behavioristic
    c. classical conditioning
    d. operant conditioning

ESSENTIAL STRATEGIES FOR SUCCESS #6

USING THE PREMACK PRINCIPLE

Now that you are studying learning theory, let's apply what you have learned to your own studying behavior. The Premack principle tells us that we can use a high frequency behavior to reinforce a low frequency one. For many students, studying is a low frequency behavior. They simply do not do it often enough or for sufficient periods of time.

Select a behavior that you really like to do and do often (a high frequency response). You might choose making a phone call to a friend, going out, working out, eating out, or even watching TV. Now comes the difficult part. You must withhold this high frequency response and only do this behavior **after** you study. Then making the call or getting the pizza becomes a reward for studying.

Using the Premack principle in this way is a good idea because you have learned that for reinforcement to be effective, it should be immediate. The other reinforcers for studying, getting good grades, graduation, and so forth are usually delayed for long periods after you have studied very hard. You may feel as if your study behavior is not reinforced at all if you don't take the reinforcement into your own hands and use the Premack principle to reward yourself.

CHAPTER 7—MEMORY

LEARNING OBJECTIVES

The following items represent the fundamental concepts that you should know when you have finished studying this chapter. Read them now as a chapter preview and return to them to test your knowledge after you have studied.

Topic A
1. Describe the information processing view of memory.
2. Discuss sensory memory, including its capacity and duration.
3. Describe how material is encoded in short-term memory and how long it is stored there.
4. Describe the role of maintenance rehearsal in retaining information in short-term memory.
5. Know how much information is held in short-term memory and how chunking affects that amount.
6. Discuss the importance of acoustic coding in short-term memory.
7. Describe the capacity and duration of long-term memory.
8. Explain how elaborative rehearsal helps to encode information in long-term memory.
9. Describe three possible types of long term memory.

Topic B
1. Explain how measures of recall and recognition affect assessment of retrieval.
2. Explain implicit and explicit tests of retention and what they tell us about long-term memory.
3. Describe the encoding specificity principle.
4. Define meaningfulness and explain how it relates to retrieval.
5. Define mnemonic devices and describe examples.
6. Define schemas and explain how they affect retrieval.
7. Define overlearning, massed practice, and distributed practice and explain how they affect retrieval.
8. Distinguish between retroactive and proactive interference and explain how each affects retrieval.

VOCABULARY CHAPTER 7

On your own paper, write the definition for each of the following key terms. Your learning will be facilitated by writing the definition in your own words rather than copying the exact definition from your text.

MEMORY	ENCODING
STORAGE	RETRIEVAL
SENSORY MEMORY	SHORT-TERM MEMORY
MAINTENANCE REHEARSAL	CHUNK
LONG-TERM MEMORY	ELABORATIVE REHEARSAL
PROCEDURAL MEMORY	SEMANTIC MEMORY
EPISODIC MEMORY	RECALL
RECOGNITION	RELEARNING
ENCODING SPECIFICITY PRINCIPLE	STATE-DEPENDENT MEMORY
FLASHBULB MEMORIES	MEANINGFULNESS
MNEMONIC DEVICES	NARRATIVE CHAINING
METHOD OF LOCI	SCHEMA
OVERLEARNING	RETROACTIVE INTERFERENCE
PROACTIVE INTERFERENCE	

MATCHING TOPIC 7A

Match the following key terms with the appropriate definition.

_____ 1. episodic memory   _____ 2. short-term memory
_____ 3. retrieval   _____ 4. chunk
_____ 5. sensory memory   _____ 6. long-term memory
_____ 7. memory   _____ 8. elaborative rehearsal
_____ 9. semantic memory   _____ 10. procedural memory
_____ 11. storage   _____ 12. maintenance rehearsal
_____ 13. encoding

a. The cognitive ability to encode, store, and retrieve information.
b. The active process of representing and putting of information into memory.
c. The process of holding encoded information in memory.
d. The process of locating, removing, and using information that is stored in memory.

88

e. The type of memory that holds large amounts of information from the senses for very brief periods of time.

f. A type of memory with limited capacity (7 plus or minus 2 bits of information) and limited duration (15-20 seconds).

g. A process of rote repetition (reattending) to keep information in short-term memory.

h. A somewhat imprecise concept, referring to a meaningful unit of information as represented in memory.

i. A type of memory with virtually unlimited capacity and very long, if not limitless, duration.

j. A mechanism for processing information into long-term memory that involves the meaningful manipulation of the information to be remembered.

k. In long-term memory, the storage of stimulus-response associations and skilled patterns of responses.

l. In long-term memory, the storage of vocabulary, facts, simple concepts, rules, and the like.

m. In long-term memory, the storage of life events and experiences.

MATCHING TOPIC 7B

Match the following key terms with the appropriate definition.

_____ 1.	method of loci	_____ 2.	proactive interference
_____ 3.	state-dependent memory	_____ 4.	mnemonic devices
_____ 5.	narrative chaining	_____ 6.	overlearning
_____ 7.	encoding specificity principle	_____ 8.	recall
_____ 9.	retroactive interference	_____ 10.	recognition
_____ 11.	meaningfulness	_____ 12.	schema
_____ 13.	flashbulb memories	_____ 14.	relearning

a. An explicit measure of retrieval in which an individual is given the fewest possible cues to retrieval.

b. An explicit measure of retrieval in which an individual is required to identify as familiar material previously learned.

c. An implicit measure of memory in which one notes an improvement in performance when learning material for a second time.

d. The hypothesis that how we retrieve information depends on how it was encoded, and that retrieval is enhanced to the extent that retrieval cues match encoding cues.

e. The notion that retrieval is enhanced to the extent that one's state of mind at retrieval matches one's state of mind at encoding.

f. Particularly clear and vivid memories--usually of emotional experiences--that are easily retrieved, but not necessarily accurate in all detail.

g. The extent to which information evokes associations with information already in memory.

h. Strategies for improving retrieval that take advantage of existing memories in order to organize information and make new material meaningful.

i. The mnemonic device of relating words together in a story, thus organizing them in a meaningful way.

j. The mnemonic device that mentally places information to be retrieved in a series of familiar locations (loci).

k. A system of organized general knowledge, stored in long-term memory, that may guide the encoding and retrieval of information.

l. The practice or rehearsal of material over and above what is needed to learn it.

m. The inhibition of retrieval of previously learned material caused by material learned later.

n. The inhibition of retrieval of recently learned material caused by material learned earlier.

TRUE-FALSE TEST TOPIC 7A

_____ 1. It would be accurate to say that the processing of information begins with sensation.

_____ 2. According to information processing theory, information must be stored before it can be retrieved.

_____ 3. Three different types of memory are: perceptual memory, short-term memory and long-term memory.

_____ 4. Sensory memory has rather large capacity, but limited duration.

_____ 5. There is evidence for sensory memory for vision and audition.

_____ 6. Another name for sensory memory is working memory.

_____ 7. Maintenance rehearsal is a good strategy for increasing the duration of short-term memory.

_____ 8. Chunking makes the capacity for short-term memory virtually limitless.

_____ 9. Research suggests that information is acoustically encoded in short-term memory.

_____ 10. Eliminating the effects of injury or illness, one could assume that certain information in long-term memory would never be forgotten.

_____ 11. The majority of psychologists agree that once information is transferred to long-term memory, it stays there till we die.

_____ 12. According to Loftus and Loftus, sometimes when we think we are remembering original events, we may actually be reconstructing the details of those memories.

_____ 13. At this time, the question of repressed memories of childhood abuse remains unanswerable by scientific research.

_____ 14. Our knowledge of how to drive a car or type a letter is referred to as episodic memory.

_____ 15. Autobiographical memory does not seem to develop until about age 10.

TRUE-FALSE TEST TOPIC 7B

_____ 1. Asking students to remember a set of history facts and assimilate them into a good essay answer is an example of recall.

_____ 2. Retrieval by recognition is always superior to retrieval by recall.

_____ 3. A multiple choice test item and an essay item would both measure retrieval by recall.

_____ 4. Recall and recognition are both explicit measures of memory.

_____ 5. Relearning generally takes as many trials or presentations of the material as the first learning.

_____ 6. Procedural memory tasks are often used as implicit measures of memory.

_____ 7. Amnesia victims seem to retain much of their procedural memory.

_____ 8. The encoding specificity principle applies only to humans.

_____ 9. According to the encoding specificity principle, when cues that were present at encoding are also present at retrieval, retrieval is enhanced.

_____ 10. According to research by Gordon Bower, even the mood a person is in when material is encoded can be an important factor for retrieval.

_____ 11. There is evidence that memories of emotionally arousing events that produce extreme anxiety may be more difficult to recall.

_____ 12. In general, the more meaningful the material to be learned, the easier it will be to recall.

_____ 13. Narrative chaining and the method of loci are both mnemonic devices.

_____ 14. Schemas must be present at encoding in order to aid retrieval.

_____ 15. Research results clearly indicate that massed practice is superior to distributed practice.

FILL-IN TEST TOPIC 7A

1. _____ is the capacity to encode, store, and retrieve information.
2. _____ memory has short duration, but large capacity.
3. Short-term memory is also called _____ memory.
4. _____ _____ is rote repetition that extends the duration of short-term memory.
5. _____ _____ introduced the idea of short-term memory being limited to 5 to 9 chunks of information.
6. _____ is the purposeful forgetting of unpleasant or traumatic events.
7. _____ argues that memories of child abuse may be planted by a therapist.
8. Vocabulary, rules, and simple concepts are stored in _____ memory.
9. Life events and experiences that are particularly important to us are stored in _____ memory.
10. According to _____, we store memories of our life events and experiences in episodic memory.

FILL-IN TEST TOPIC 7B

1. _____ tasks provide the fewest possible cues to aid retrieval.
2. _____ tasks require a subject to simply identify previously learned material.
3. _____ is an implicit test of memory indicating that learning material a second time takes less effort than the first time .
4. _____ memories seem resistant to destruction even by such problems as amnesia.

5. How-to-study-in-college books often recommend studying in one special place. The theoretical basis for this bit of wisdom is related to the _____ _____ principle.

6. Memories of important events that are especially clear and vivid are called _____ memories.

7. _____ found that retrieval is best when the mood at retrieval matched the mood at encoding.

8. _____ resides in the memory of the learner, not in the content or nature of the material being learned.

9. Aids to retrieval that help organize material and make it meaningful are called _____ _____.

10. _____ _____ is a technique by which information is organized into a meaningful story.

11. _____ provide a framework through which we understand and retrieve information.

12. The process of practicing or rehearsing material over and above what is needed to learn it is called _____.

13. When interfering activities follow the material to be learned, the interference is called _____.

MULTIPLE CHOICE TEST TOPIC 7A

1. The type of memory with large capacity and brief duration is
   a. sensory memory.
   b. short-term memory.
   c. working memory.
   d. long-term memory.

2. Which of the following represents the correct sequence of events for the process of memory?
   a. encoding-retrieving-storing
   b. storing-retrieving-encoding
   c. retrieving-storing-encoding
   d. encoding-storing-retrieving

3. Which type of memory has both the greatest capacity and the longest duration?
   a. sensory memory
   b. short-term memory
   c. long-term memory
   d. working memory

4. Repeating a person's name over and over immediately after being introduced is an example of
   a. chunking.
   b. elaboration.
   c. a mnemonic device.
   d. maintenance rehearsal.

5. When information is stored or represented by sound, it is in our _____ memory.
   a. short-term
   b. long-term
   c. sensory
   d. metamemory

6. In regard to long-term memory, most psychologists believe that
   a. all information stored in long-term memory is there until we die.
   b. long term memories are largely reconstructions from the original information.
   c. people don't remember anything that happened before age three.
   d. memory failure involves permanent forgetting, not just retrieval failure.

7. To store information in long-term memory, one should use
   a. attention.
   b. maintenance rehearsal.
   c. elaborative rehearsal.
   d. repetition.

8. Your memory of the definition of psychology is stored in
   a. episodic memory.
   b. metamemory.
   c. semantic memory.
   d. procedural memory.

9. The capacity of short-term memory can be increased through
   a. chunking.
   b. attention.
   c. rehearsal.
   d. selective encoding.

10. A person's memory of his/her first date would be stored in _____ memory.
   a. semantic
   b. autobiographical
   c. metamemory
   d. procedural

MULTIPLE CHOICE TEST TOPIC 7B

1. Which of the following is NOT a correct match?
   a. fill-in test item - recall
   b. multiple choice test item - recognition
   c. essay test item - recognition
   d. true-false test item - recognition

2. According to your text, the best place to study for an exam in this course is in the classroom where the test will be administered. This is best explained by the
   a. quiet surroundings.
   b. encoding specificity principle.
   c. availability of tutors.
   d. principle of state dependent learning.

3. Words like angel, redwood, and vehicle are easier to retrieve than words like political, religious, and betrayal because
   a. they are shorter words.
   b. they are more meaningful words.
   c. they lend themselves better to the use of mental images.
   d. they don't require elaborative rehearsal techniques to transfer to long-term memory.

4. Which of the following types of memory is most resistant to destruction?
   a. episodic memory
   b. metamemory
   c. semantic memory
   d. procedural memory

5. Which of the following is TRUE of amnesia victims?
   a. They have probably lost all of their procedural memory.
   b. They will perform as well as nonvictims on implicit measures of memory.
   c. They will be unable to experience flashbulb memories.
   d. Their sensory memory will be impaired.

6. Research by Gordon Bower suggests that
   a. retrieval is not related to context.
   b. one's mood can predict retrieval.
   c. retrieval is enhanced by positive moods.
   d. retrieval is worse under the influence of drugs.

7. Research on flashbulb memories indicates that they are
   a. no more accurate or complete than other memories.
   b. less reliable than procedural memories.
   c. especially susceptible to the effects of amnesia.
   d. recalled less easily in the presence of a person who shared the event.

8. Which of the following is NOT a mnemonic device?
   a. method of loci
   b. narrative chaining
   c. elaborative rehearsal
   d. key word method

9. If you prepare for your next psychology exam by studying for several short periods separated by rest periods or breaks, you are using
   a. massed practice.
   b. distributed practice.
   c. cramming.
   d. elaborative rehearsal.

10. Chess players are able to remember in great detail the positions of chess pieces on a chess board as long as the positions are related to actual chess games. The best explanation for this is their use of
    a. massed practice.
    b. schemas.
    c. the encoding specificity principle.
    d. mnemonic devices.

11. Which of the following factors influences the impact of interference on learning?
    a. the nature of the material being learned
    b. the organization and meaningfulness of the information learned
    c. the type of activity that follows studying
    d. all of the above

12. A student who has studied German in high school, takes a course in French in college and now has trouble remembering the German. This is an example of the effects of
    a. retroactive interference.
    b. proactive interference.
    c. state-dependent learning.
    d. encoding specificity.

ESSENTIAL STRATEGIES FOR SUCCESS #7

USING MNEMONIC STRATEGIES AS STUDY METHODS

Some concepts related to the material in Chapter 7 can be directly applied to study methods. For example, the serial position effect tells us that when we study a series, the natural tendency is that the items at the beginning and end of the series will be easiest to learn. Our application should be to study the information in the middle of a chapter or in the middle of our notes a little more thoroughly to offset the serial position effect.

The concepts of state-dependent and context-dependent recall have some application to studying. State-dependent recall tells us that for optimum recall, we should take the test in the same state we were in when we learned the material. Context-dependent recall tells us that the setting actually serves as a cue. I sometimes suggest that my students return to their empty classroom in the afternoons and spend time studying psychology there. After all, it is the context in which they will take their exams.

We can also use other ideas such as the concept of chunking. Many mnemonic strategies employ this technique to create greater memory capacity. For instance, you may have learned this mnemonic to help you remember the order of operations in algebra: "Please excuse my dear Aunt Sally," or PEMDAS. This chunk forms a cue to help us remember to solve algebraic equations by attending to P = parenthesis, E = exponents, M = multiply, D = divide, A = add, and S = subtract in that order. Many of these mnemonics already exist, FACE tells us the notes on the spaces of the music scale and HOMES reminds us of the names of the great lakes, Huron, Ontario, Michigan, Erie, and Superior.

You may use other mnemonics that you have learned, but you can also create your own. If the letters do not conveniently spell a word, such as HOMES or FACE, simply form a chunk by creating a sentence that uses words beginning with the appropriate letters. For example, rehearsal, elaboration, and chunking are ways of extending the length of time that information stays in short-term memory. The first letters of these words are r, e, and c. You might put these into a sentence such as "Rats eat cheese."

Mnemonic devices work even better when you create your own because you are processing the information while making the mnemonic. Try creating your own using some information from your text.

If you are intrigued by the idea of improving your memory and would like to know more, I recommend a small paperback book by Harry Lorraine and Jerry Lucas called, The Memory Book. I am confident that you can find other excellent sources of information on memory in the library.

CHAPTER 8—HIGHER COGNITIVE PROCESSES

LEARNING OBJECTIVES

The following items represent the fundamental concepts that you should know when you have finished studying this chapter. Read them now as a chapter preview and return to them to test your knowledge after you have studied.

Topic A
1. List three components of a problem.
2. Explain how to distinguish between problems that are well-defined or ill-defined.
3. Describe problem representation.
4. Discuss how algorithmic and heuristic strategies are used to solve problems.
5. Define mental set and explain how it affects problem-solving.
6. Define functional fixedness and describe its affects on problem-solving.
7. Contrast divergent thinking and convergent thinking.

Topic B
1. List the defining characteristics of language.
2. Discuss the use of language as a social process.
3. Describe the landmark events that occur during language acquisition.
4. Explain the learning-oriented and biology-oriented theories of language acquisition.

Topic C
1. Understand the operational definition of intelligence.
2. Define psychological test.
3. Differentiate between test reliability and test validity.
4. Define norms and understand their use in psychological testing.
5. Describe the development of the Stanford-Binet Intelligence Test and describe the Wechsler Intelligence Scales.
6. Describe Terman's study of gifted individuals, including selection, problems, and results.
7. List six ways in which individuals can be considered to be gifted.
8. Define mental retardation and discuss its causes, treatment, and prevention.
9. Describe Down's syndrome and phenylketonuria.

VOCABULARY CHAPTER 8

On your own paper, write the definition for each of the following key terms. Your learning will be facilitated by writing the definition in your own words rather than copying the exact definition from your text.

PROBLEM	STRATEGY
ALGORITHM	HEURISTIC
MENTAL SET	FUNCTIONAL FIXEDNESS
DIVERGENT THINKING	CONVERGENT THINKING
PSYCHOLINGUISTICS	LANGUAGE
PRAGMATICS	BABBLING
HOLOPHRASTIC SPEECH	TELEGRAPHIC SPEECH
OVERREGULATIZATION	INTELLIGENCE
PSYCHOLOGICAL TEST	RELIABILITY
VALIDITY	NORMS
g	IQ
MENTAL RETARDATION	DOWN'S SYNDROME
PHENYLKETONURIA	

MATCHING TOPICS 8A, B, C

Match the following key terms with the appropriate definition.

_____ 1.	overregularization	_____ 2.	holophrastic speech
_____ 3.	psycholinguistics	_____ 4.	language
_____ 5.	mental retardation	_____ 6.	Down's syndrome
_____ 7.	phenylketonuria	_____ 8.	babbling
_____ 9.	convergent thinking	_____ 10.	problem
_____ 11.	mental set	_____ 12.	divergent thinking
_____ 13.	strategy	_____ 14.	functional fixedness
_____ 15.	g	_____ 16.	heuristic
_____ 17.	reliability	_____ 18.	intelligence
_____ 19.	psychological test	_____ 20.	validity
_____ 21.	norms	_____ 22.	pragmatics
_____ 23.	IQ	_____ 24.	telegraphic speech
_____ 25.	algorithm		

a. A situation in which there is a discrepancy between one's current state and one's desired, or goal state, with no clear way of getting from one to the other.

b. In problem-solving, a systematic plan for generating possible solutions that can be tested to see if they are correct.

c. A problem-solving strategy in which all possible solutions are generated and tested and an acceptable solution is guaranteed.

d. A problem-solving strategy in which hypotheses about problem solutions are generated and tested in a time-saving and systematic way, but does not guarantee an acceptable solution.

e. A predisposed (set) way to perceive something; an expectation.

f. The phenomenon in which one is unable to see a new use or function for an object because of experience using the object in some other function.

g. The creation of many ideas or potential problem solutions from one idea.

h. The reduction or focusing of many different ideas into one possible problem solution.

i. A collection of arbitrary symbols that follow certain rules of combination and that have significance for a language-using community.

j. Speech sounds produced in rhythmic, repetitive patterns.

k. The use of one word to communicate a number of different meanings.

l. The excessive application of an acquired language rule (e.g. for plurals or past tense) in a situation where it is not appropriate.

m. The capacity to understand the world and the resourcefulness to cope with its challenges; that which an intelligence test measures.

n. An objective, standardized measure of a sample of behavior.

o. Consistency or dependability; in testing, consistency of test scores.

p. A hybrid scientific discipline of psychologists and linguists who study all aspects of language.

q. In testing, the extent to which a test measures what it claims to be measuring.

r. In the context of psychological testing, results of a test taken by a large group of subjects whose scores can be used to make comparisons or give meaning to new scores.

s. Below average general intellectual functioning which began before the age of 18 and is associated with maladaptive behaviors.

t. A condition of many symptoms including mental retardation, caused by an extra (47th) chromosome.

u. A genetically caused disorder that produces mental retardation and that is now detectable and preventable.

v. Literally, intelligence quotient: the results of dividing one's mental age by one's chronological age, and multiplying the dividend by 100.

w. On an intelligence test, a measure of one's overall, general intellectual abilites comMonly thought of as IQ.

x. Spoken language consisting of nouns, verbs, adjectives, and adverbs, but few "function words."

y. The study of how linguistic events and their interpretation are related to the context in which they occur.

TRUE-FALSE TEST TOPIC 8A

_____ 1. The first step in problem solving is simply recognizing that a problem exists.

_____ 2. The problems we face in everyday life are usually well-defined ones.

_____ 3. Problem representation can be a major stumbling block to solving the problem.

_____ 4. The use of strategies gives the problem solver some sense of control over tasks.

_____ 5. Algorithms and heuristics are two problem-solving barriers.

_____ 6. Mental set and functional fixedness are just two names for the same thing.

_____ 7. There is a strong correlation between creative problem solving and intelligence.

_____ 8. Divergent thinking is generally more useful for creative problem solving than convergent thinking.

_____ 9. Generating as many uses as possible for a common object is a simple test for convergent thinking.

_____ 10. Creative problem-solving involves preparation, incubation, illumination, and verification.

TRUE-FALSE TEST TOPIC 8B

_____ 1. Language can be thought of as a large set of symbols.

_____ 2. An adult speaking "baby talk" is demonstrating the pragmatics of language.

_____ 3. There are no gender-based differences in language usage.

_____ 4. Language acquisition is considered a significant achievement in childhood.

_____ 5. Holophrastic speech precedes telegraphic speech.

_____ 6. Most babies speak in two-word phrases by age one.

_____ 7. Overregularization provides evidence in support of the learning theory of language acquisition.

_____ 8. We acquire some notion of word meanings through classical conditioning.

_____ 9. Skinner suggested the notion of the language acquisition device.

_____ 10. The best position on language acquisition is an interactionist view crediting both the learning and the biological theories.

TRUE-FALSE TEST TOPIC 8C

_____ 1. Defining intelligence as "that which intelligence tests measure" is an example of an operational definition.

_____ 2. A psychological test should be a standardized, objective test.

_____ 3. A psychological test should be viewed as a sample of behavior.

_____ 4. General intellectual ability consists of convergent and divergent thinking.

_____ 5. The usefulness of a psychological test often depends on the adequacy of the norms used to make comparisons of scores.

_____ 6. Fluid-analytic abilities are related to formal schooling.

_____ 7. Lewis Terman wrote the first intelligence test.

_____ 8. The Stanford-Binet intelligence test was the basis for the first calculation of IQ.

_____ 9. The WAIS-R is an intelligence test for children.

_____ 10. Down syndrome and PKU are two causes of mental retardation.

FILL-IN TEST TOPIC 8A

1. A _____ problem is one in which the initial state and the goal state are clearly defined.

2. A systematic plan for generating possible problem solutions that can be tested is called a/an _____.

3. A/an _____ is a problem-solving strategy that guarantees that you will eventually arrive at a solution.

4. Mental set and functional fixedness are both _____ to problem solving.

5. Starting with one idea and generating from it a number of alternative possibilities is _____ thinking.
6. In the _____ stage of creative problem solving, the basic elements of the problem are considered.
7. In the _____ stage of creative problem solving, a potential solution seems to appear as if from nowhere.

FILL-IN TEST TOPIC 8B

1. _____ is a discipline of scientists trained in both psychology and linguistics.
2. Language consists of a large number of _____.
3. _____ is the study of how linguistic events are related to the social context in which they occur.
4. _____ is the production of speech sounds in repetitive, rhythmic patterns.
5. The use of just one word to communicate a range of intentions and meanings is referred to as _____ speech.
6. _____ is the continued application of an acquired language rule in situations where it is not appropriate.
7. _____ suggested the existence of the language acquisition device.
8. Two potential theories of language acquisition are the learning theory and the _____ theory.

FILL-IN TEST TOPIC 8C

1. A psychological test must be standardized and _____.
2. Consistency or dependability in a psychological test is referred to as _____.
3. The extent to which a test actually measures what it claims to measure is called _____.
4. Results of a test taken by a large group of subjects whose scores can be used to make comparisons are called _____.
5. The author of the first intelligence test was _____ _____.

6. _____ abilities represent skills needed for problem solving.

7. One of the most commonly used of all psychological tests is the _____.

8. The psychologist who contributed most to our knowledge of gifted individuals was _____.

9. The term mentally retarded is being replaced with the term _____ _____.

10. _____ _____ is a genetic cause of mental retardation characterized by the presence of a 47th chromosome.

11. In 1994, a controversial book titled ____ _____ _____ reignited the feud over racial differences in IQ.

12. In 1969, _____ _____ argued that racial differences in IQ are due to genetic factors.

MULTIPLE CHOICE TEST TOPIC 8A

1. Deciding on a career path would be an example of a/an
   a. unsolvable problem.
   b. ill-defined problem.
   c. well-defined problem
   d. common problem.

2. Which of the following is NOT one of the major components of a problem?
   a. initial state
   b. goal state
   c. incubation state
   d. possible solutions

3. An informal, rule-of-thumb method for generating and testing problem solutions defines a/an
   a. heuristic.
   b. algorithm.
   c. mental set.
   d. strategy.

4. Which of the following are barriers to effective problems solving?
   a. inability to think divergently
   b. mental set
   c. functional fixedness
   d. all of the above

5. A motorist returning from the grocery store is stuck on an icy patch of roadway. The car will not move in any direction, as the tires spin freely on the ice. A passenger takes a bag of "kitty litter" from a grocery sack and spreads it on the ice under the tires, thus freeing the car. The driver is impressed, and claims that he never would have thought of doing that, thus demonstrating
   a. poor problem representation..
   b. functional fixedness.
   c. the availability heuristic.
   d. divergent thinking.

6. The fictional detective, Sherlock Holmes, was well-known for his ability to observe many different clues and use them to solve a difficult mystery. His ability demonstrates
   a. divergent thinking.
   b. convergent thinking.
   c. availability heuristic.
   d. means-end analysis.

7. Working a crossword puzzle would be an example of a/an
   a. unsolvable problem.
   b. ill-defined problem.
   c. well-defined problem.
   d. common problem.

8. Joe has a problem. He is unemployed. He knows that his goal is to get a job. However, he has no idea how to begin finding employment. We might say that his problem solving skills have broken down at the _____ stage.
   a. initial
   b. goal
   c. routes or strategies
   d. solutions

9. During which stage of creative problem solving is the person the least engaged in thinking about the problem?
   a. preparation
   b. incubation
   c. illumination
   d. verification

10. During which stage of creative problem solving is the actual solution likely to occur?
    a. preparation
    b. incubation
    c. illumination
    d. verification

MULTIPLE CHOICE TEST TOPIC 8B

1. Which of the following is NOT part of the definition of language?
   a. rules of combination
   b. symbols
   c. sounds
   d. language community

2. Psycholinguists might study
   a. pragmatics.
   b. PKU.
   c. functional fixedness.
   d. the WAIS-R.

3. Pragmatics involves decisions about language based on
   a. the intelligence of the listener.
   b. the social context of the situation.
   c. the vocabulary of the speaker.
   d. none of the above.

4. In regard to gender differences in language usage, which of the following statements is TRUE?
   a. Men are more talkative than women and tend to interrupt more.
   b. Men are shy and talk less about themselves than women.
   c. Men use more qualifiers than women do.
   d. Men are more likely to express their feelings than women.

5. Which of the following represents the correct sequence in language acquisition?
   a. babbling, telegraphic speech, holophrastic speech
   b. telegraphic speech, holophrastic speech, babbling
   c. telegraphic speech, babbling, holophrastic speech
   d. babbling, holophrastic speech, telegraphic speech

6. A baby's first words are usually produced at about age
   a. six months.
   b. nine months.
   c. twelve months.
   d. eighteen months.

7. Which of the following statements concerning language development is/are TRUE?
   a. Parents correct the content rather than the form in their children's language.
   b. Parents do not reinforce language learning.
   c. Vocabulary cannot be learned from models.
   d. all of the above.

8. The language acquisition device is most appropriately associated with the
   a. biological theory of language acquisition.
   b. learning theory of language acquisition.
   c. pragmatics of language.
   d. problem of overregularization.

MULTIPLE CHOICE TEST TOPIC 8C

1. A psychological test can measure
   a. behavior.
   b. aptitudes.
   c. feelings.
   d. all of the above.

2. If a test is administered in such a way that all who take the test get the same instructions, the same time limits, and virtually the same testing conditions, we say that the test is
   a. objective.
   b. standardized.
   c. valid.
   d. reliable.

3. To qualify as a good psychological test, an instrument should have
   a. reliability.
   b. validity.
   c. adequate norms.
   d. all of the above.

4. A psychologist working in a rehabilitation center needs to know the "IQ" of a single adult client. The best test to use would be the
   a. WAIS-R.
   b. WISC-R.
   c. Stanford-Binet.
   d. OLSAT.

5. Which of the following is NOT one of the three levels of cognitive ability assessed by the Stanford Binet?
   a. crystallized abilities
   b. fluid-analytic abilities
   c. reading comprehension abilities
   d. short-term memory

6. Which of the following is NOT one of the problems associated with Lewis Terman's research on gifted individuals?
   a. failing to control for factors such as socioeconomic level or parent's education level
   b. using too narrow a definition for giftedness
   c. failing to include black children
   d. excluding children who had psychological problems

7. According to the AAMD, the definition of mental retardation should include
   a. only individuals whose IQ is lower than 70.
   b. some measure of a person's ability to adapt to the environment.
   c. only a deficiency in skills measured by IQ tests.
   d. the 5 percent of the population with the lowest IQ scores.

8. Perhaps the greatest hope in dealing with mental retardation is in the area of
   a. increasing the IQ of the profoundly retarded.
   b. curing Down's syndrome.
   c. preventing retardation by learning more about the prenatal environment.
   d. redefining retardation so that fewer individuals are labeled.

9. PKU is treated by
   a. drugs.
   b. radiation.
   c. diet.
   d. physical therapy.

10. _____ is a form of mental retardation with a genetic basis found primarily in males, who characteristically have long faces, big ears, and, as adults, large testes.
    a. Down syndrome
    b. PKU
    c. fetal alcohol syndrome
    d. fragile X syndrome

11. Arthur Jensen argued that black/white differences in IQ scores could be attributed to
    a. environmental factors.
    b. genetic factors.
    c. cultural differences.
    d. test bias.

12. Our most important concern relative to differences in IQ should be
    a. determining whether the differences are genetic.
    b. focusing on gender differences.
    c. determining whether IQ can be changed.
    d. discovering which environmental factors are involved.

ESSENTIAL STRATEGIES FOR SUCCESS #8

GETTING ALONG WITH YOUR PROFESSOR

Although your grade may not depend on it, you may enjoy your class more and learn more if you create a positive relationship with the instructor. Research on adult thinking indicates that a college education is a very influential factor in cognitive development and that interacting with professors is one of the key influences. Here are some do's and don'ts that will help you get along and create a positive impression.

DO'S:

1. Learn the professor's name and appropriate title.
2. Attend every class and <u>be on time</u>.
3. Make an appointment to visit your professor during office hours. Express an interest in the course and in your grades. Learn about the professor's interests.
4. Prepare for class by reading assignments ahead so that you can answer and ask informed questions.
5. Sit near the front of the room or down the center aisles.
6. Inform your professor of any special problems or needs you may have. For example, if you are epileptic or have hearing or vision problems, the instructor should be informed.

DON'TS:

1. Don't do anything that will call negative attention to yourself such as talking at inappropriate times or being late to class repeatedly.
2. If you miss class, NEVER ask, "Did we do anything in class today?"
3. Do not confess to the instructor that you have not read the assignments or are not prepared for class and do not offer excuses.
4. Do not miss an exam unless you are absolutely too ill to walk into the room and in that event, try to let the instructor know ahead of time that you cannot be there.
5. Don't be afraid to approach your professor with concerns about class—most of us are human.

CHAPTER 9—MOTIVATION AND EMOTION

LEARNING OBJECTIVES

The following items represent the fundamental concepts that you should know when you have finished studying this chapter. Read them now as a chapter preview and return to them to test your knowledge after you have studied.

Topic A
1. Define motivation and discuss how instincts, drives, and incentives explain motivated behaviors.
2. Explain how the concept of balance or equilibrium can be used to explain motivated behaviors.
3. Discuss cognitive dissonance theory.
4. Explain how your body regulates its temperature.
5. List the factors that may influence thirst and hunger.
6. Describe the ways in which the sex drive is a unique physiological drive.
7. Define homosexuality and discuss the possible causes.
8. Discuss achievement motivation and explain how it is measured.
9. Discuss the needs for power and affiliation.

Topic B
1. List four components that define emotional experience.
2. Discuss the classification of emotions.
3. Describe the role of the autonomic nervous system during states of emotionality.
4. Describe the various brain centers and the role that each plays in producing emotions.
5. Discuss the relationship between facial expressions and emotion.

VOCABULARY CHAPTER 9

On your own paper, write the definition for each of the following key terms. Your learning will be facilitated by writing the definition in your own words rather than copying the exact definition from your text.

MOTIVATION   AROUSAL
INSTINCTS   NEED

DRIVE   INCENTIVES
SECONDARY DRIVE   HOMEOSTASIS
COGNITIVE DISSONANCE   HYPOTHALAMUS
NEED TO ACHIEVE   THEMATIC APPERCEPTION TEST
NEED FOR POWER   NEED FOR AFFILIATION
HOMOSEXUALS   EMOTION

MATCHING TOPICS 9A, B, C

Match the following key terms with the appropriate definition.

_____ 1. cognitive dissonance   _____ 2. need for affiliation
_____ 3. motivation   _____ 4. emotion
_____ 5. homosexuals   _____ 6. arousal
_____ 7. need for power   _____ 8. incentives
_____ 9. secondary drive   _____ 10. thematic apperception test
_____ 11. drive   _____ 12. instincts
_____ 13. hypothalamus   _____ 14. need to achieve
_____ 15. need   _____ 16. homeostasis

a. The process of arousing, maintaining, and directing behavior.

b. One's level of activation or excitement.

c. Unlearned, complex patterns of behavior that occur in the presence of particular stimuli.

d. A lack or shortage of some biological essential resulting from deprivation.

e. A state of tension resulting from a need that arouses and directs an organism's behavior.

f. External stimuli that an organism may be motivated to approach or avoid.

g. A state of balance or equilibrium among internal, physiological conditions.

h. A discomforting, motivating state that occurs when one's ideas or beliefs are not in balance or equilibrium.

i. A small midbrain structure near the limbic system associated with feeding, drinking, temperature regulation, sex, and aggression.

j. The learned need to meet or exceed some standard of excellence in performance.

k. A projective personality test requiring a subject to tell a series of short stories about a set of ambiguous pictures.

l. The learned need to be in control of events or persons, usually at another's expense.

m. The need to be with others and to form relationships and associations.

114

n. Persons who are attracted to and sexually aroused by members of their own sex.

o. A reaction involving subjective feeling, physiological response, cognitive interpretation, and behavioral expression.

p. Arousers and directors of behaviors that stem from learned, or acquired, needs that are not tied to one's biological survival.

TRUE-FALSE TEST TOPIC 9A

_____ 1. In the 1800s, psychologists explained behavior in terms of conscious motivation.

_____ 2. Both William James and William McDougall supported the notion that human behavior, like that of animals, is based on instincts.

_____ 3. The problem with explaining human behavior with lists of instincts is that even though the lists grew, nothing was really being explained.

_____ 4. Clark Hull postulated a theory of motivation based on fear and pain avoidance.

_____ 5. All human drives seem to be based on biological needs.

_____ 6. Maslow arranged human needs in a hierarchy beginning with physiological needs.

_____ 7. Cannon's idea of set point applies only to basal metabolism rate.

_____ 8. Arousal theory suggests that all people operate best at the same level of arousal.

_____ 9. Hebb used the term cognitive dissonance to describe a state of tension or discomfort existing when one has inconsistent cognitions.

_____ 10. Temperature, thirst, and hunger are physiologically based drives.

_____ 11. The hypothalamus plays a role in our experience of hunger.

_____ 12. Anorexia and bulimia are just two names for the same eating disorder.

_____ 13. One interesting thing about anorexia nervosa is its predominance among females.

_____ 14. With treatment, the prognosis for patients with eating disorders is very good.

_____ 15. As the complexity of the organism increases, from rats to dogs to humans, the role of internal cues in the sex drive becomes less important.

_____ 16. Dr. Simon LeVay has found evidence of a biological correlate of homosexuality.

_____ 17. Both power needs and the need for achievement are measured by the TAT.

_____ 18. It would be unusual for a person to be high in both need for power and need for affiliation.

TRUE-FALSE TEST TOPIC 9B

_____ 1. Emotions are generally unrelated to motivation.

_____ 2. Wilhelm Wundt classified emotions along three dimensions.

_____ 3. Izard, Plutchik, and Lazarus are three psychologists currently working on classifying emotions.

_____ 4. Ortony and Turner suggest that psychologists should not be concerned with identifying the basic emotions.

_____ 5. The peripheral nervous system is most involved in the physiological responses to emotion.

_____ 6. The two brain structures most involved in emotionality are the hypothalamus and the reticular activating system.

_____ 7. The role of the cerebral cortex in emotionality is mostly excitatory.

_____ 8. Humans are the only animals that outwardly express emotions.

_____ 9. There appears to be a great deal of agreement across cultures as to the relationship between facial expressions and emotions.

_____ 10. Research suggests that simply moving one's face into a position associated with the expression of a particular emotion can bring about that emotion.

FILL-IN TEST TOPIC 9A

1. _____refers to a person's level of activation or excitement.
2. Unlearned, complex patterns of behavior that occur in the presence of certain stimuli are _____.
3. _____ was the psychologist whose need/drive theory of motivation was dominant in the 1940s.
4. Being motivated to work for money is an example of a _____ drive.

116

5. A homeless person holding a sign "will work for food" is motivated by a _____ drive.

6. According to _____, the needs that motivate human behavior are limited in number and arranged in a hierarchy.

7. According to Maslow, the ultimate need is for _____ _____.

8. If we succumb to the temptations of the dessert menu, we are feeling the pull of an _____.

9. A person's most suitable or normal level of activity for certain functions is called _____ _____.

10. Zuckerman refers to people who need very high levels of arousal as _____ _____.

11. A basically honest person who cheats "just once" on his or her taxes may experience _____ _____.

12. _____ is an eating disorder characterized by repeated episodes of binge eating and purging.

13. _____ _____ developed the TAT as a means for measuring the need for achievement.

14. Women who were said to back off from competition for fear of winning and thus losing popularity and femininity were said to be suffering from _____ ____ _____.

15. The need to form friendships and associations is known as the need for _____.

FILL-IN TEST TOPIC 9B

1. The subjective feeling component of emotion is also referred to as _____.

2. _____ was the first psychologist to attempt to classify emotions.

3. _____ is developing a classification theory of emotions that emphasizes the role of motivation.

4. _____ and _____ argue against trying to classify emotions.

5. After emotional arousal, the _____ division of the autonomic nervous system helps return your body's functions to normal levels.

6. _____ _____ has been helpful in identifying the role of the brain in emotional arousal.

7. _____ was one of the first to popularize the idea of a relationship between facial expression and emotional state.

8. _____ has focused his study of facial expression on cultural differences.

MULTIPLE CHOICE TEST TOPIC 9A

1. A problem with using instincts to explain human behavior is that
   a. it makes human behavior seem too much like animal behavior.
   b. the list of instincts becomes unmanageable.
   c. this approach simply renames the behaviors and doesn't really explain anything.
   d. humans don't have instincts.

2. Which of the following is an example of a secondary drive?
   a. A baby is crying because it is hungry.
   b. A toddler goes to the refrigerator and asks for "drink."
   c. An adolescent girl tells her mother she needs a new pair of shoes.
   d. A ten year old has a fever and asks his mother for aspirin.

3. Which of the following psychologists developed the need/drive theory of motivation?
   a. Clark Hull
   b. Abraham Maslow
   c. Robert Plutchik
   d. Walter Cannon

4. Which of the following situations is best explained by set point theory?
   a. A person feels bored and so he goes and takes a nap.
   b. A person climbs a mountain because it is there.
   c. A person does a job so he will get paid.
   d. A person loses weight while ill and then quickly gains it back.

5. Which of the following is NOT part of Maslow's hierarchy of needs?
   a. safety needs
   b. love and belongingness
   c. affiliation needs
   d. self-actualization

6. Which of the following psychologists is associated with cognitive dissonance theory?
   a. Cannon
   b. Zuckerman
   c. Maslow
   d. Festinger

7. The body's centers for regulating temperature are both located in the
   a. cerebral cortex.
   b. hypothalamus.
   c. parasympathetic nervous system.
   d. limbic system.

8. Our most important physiological cues for eating come from
   a. the liver and the hypothalamus.
   b. stomach contractions.
   c. the sight of food.
   d. the smell of food.

9. The prognosis for anorexia nervosa is particularly poor with almost _____ percent relapsing within a year of the end of treatment.
   a. 20
   b. 35
   c. 50
   d. 60

10. Which of the following statements regarding the prognosis and treatment of eating disorders is TRUE?
   a. Bulimia has a far worse prognosis than anorexia.
   b. The prognosis for bulimia is better with family therapy than with individual therapy.
   c. Anti-depressant drugs are unsuccessful with both disorders.
   d. Hospitalization is usually required for treating both disorders.

11. Which of the following is NOT one of the ways in which the sex drive differs from other physiologically based drives?
   a. The survival of the individual does not depend on the sex drive.
   b. The sex drive tends to deplete the body's resources whereas other drives replenish the body.
   c. The sex drive is not present at birth.
   d. The sex drive is never satisfied completely.

12. Which of the following is the best explanation for homosexuality?
    a. It is the result of environmental influences.
    b. It may be the result of environmental or genetic influences but no one really knows for sure.
    c. It appears to run in families so it must be genetically determined.
    d. It is caused by a hormonal imbalance during prenatal development.

13. Which of the following is NOT true of homosexuality?
    a. Homosexuals experience a pattern of responsiveness similar to that of heterosexuals.
    b. Most homosexuals have experienced heterosexual sex.
    c. Homosexuals have significantly different hormone levels than heterosexuals.
    d. There is now evidence of a biological correlate to homosexuality.

14. Research by David McClelland on his concept of "need to achieve" would predict that someone with a high nAch, if given a choice, would choose a job
    a. in which he or she was almost bound to be successful.
    b. that was challenging, but could be done well with effort.
    c. that was so difficult that it almost certainly could not be done well.
    d. in which he or she could succeed, but only at the expense of others.

15. The Thematic Apperception Test was developed to measure the need for
    a. achievement.
    b. competence.
    c. power.
    d. affiliation.

MULTIPLE CHOICE TEST TOPIC 9B

1. Which of the following is NOT one of the components of emotional reaction?
    a. objective feeling
    b. cognitive reaction
    c. physiological reaction
    d. behavior

2. Which of the following psychologists did NOT develop a classification system for emotions?
   a. Plutchik
   b. Lazarus
   c. Izard
   d. Murray

3. Which of the following actions would NOT result from being in an emotional situation?
   a. heart rate and blood pressure are elevated
   b. blood will clot less easily
   c. blood sugar levels increase
   d. respiration increases, making breathing deeper and more rapid

4. The part of the brain involved in the cognitive aspect of emotion is the
   a. hypothalamus.
   b. amygdala.
   c. limbic system.
   d. cerebral cortex.

5. The part of the brain involved in emotional responses for attacking or defending is the
   a. cerebral cortex.
   b. amygdala.
   c. limbic system.
   d. hypothalamus.

6. Ekman's study of the relationship between facial expression and emotional states has centered around
   a. nonhuman subjects.
   b. communication between humans and animals.
   c. racial differences in facial expression.
   d. cultural differences.

ESSENTIAL STRATEGIES FOR SUCCESS #9

TAKING OBJECTIVE TESTS

1. Read instructions carefully and follow them.
2. Read through the test and answer the questions you know immediately because this will give you a sense of confidence.
3. Once you have answered a question, NEVER change your answer unless you have a sudden insight and know another answer to be correct. Do not change just because you have begun to feel doubtful about your first response.
4. Use other questions to answer or at least give you hints about the questions you don't know.
5. On multiple choice exams, a good approach is to read only the statement and treat it as a fill in the blank question, generating your own response. Then try to find the alternative that best matches your own answer.
6. Read all multiple choice options carefully before you mark an answer.
7. Pay close attention to words such as not, never, true, false, except, always, and only.
8. On true/false exams, guess true if you have no idea at all. It is more difficult to construct false statements, and studies show that the probability of true statements is higher than that for false statements.
9. Always answer every question, even if you just make a wild guess. You will surely get no credit if you leave an answer blank.
10. The absolute best test-taking skill is preparation. Studying will do more for your exam grades than any other suggestion or tip that you can employ.

CHAPTER 10—PERSONALITY: THEORIES AND ASSESSMENT

LEARNING OBJECTIVES

The following items represent the fundamental concepts that you should know when you have finished studying this chapter. Read them now as a chapter preview and return to them to test your knowledge after you have studied.

Topic A
1. Discuss Freud's psychoanalytic theory, including levels of consciousness, life instincts and death instincts, Freud's three structures of personality, defense mechanisms, and the stages of psychosexual development.
2. Describe the contributions of Adler, Jung, and Horney to the psychoanalytic approach.
3. Discuss the strengths and weaknesses of the psychoanalytic approach.
4. Describe the personality theories of Watson, Skinner, Dollard and Miller, and Bandura, including strengths and weaknesses of the behavioral-learning approach.
5. Discuss the humanistic-phenomenological approach of Rogers and Maslow, including strengths and weaknesses.
6. Discuss the trait approach and the contributions of Allport and Cattell.
7. Define personality trait.
8. List the "Big Five" personality dimensions.
9. Discuss the strengths and weaknesses of the trait approach to personality.

Topic B
1. List the goals of personality assessment.
2. Describe how behavioral observations are used for assessing personality.
3. Discuss the advantages and disadvantages of the interview as a personality assessment technique.
4. Describe the MMPI and define multiphasic.
5. Describe the Rorschach and the TAT and discuss the characteristics of projective techniques.

VOCABULARY CHAPTER 10

On your own paper, write the definition for each of the following key terms. Your learning will be facilitated by writing the definition in your own words rather than just copying the exact definition from your text.

THEORY

PSYCHOANALYTIC APPROACH

DEATH INSTINCTS (THANATOS)

PLEASURE PRINCIPLE

REALITY PRINCIPLE

IDEALISTIC PRINCIPLE

REPRESSION

RATIONALIZATION

PROJECTION

DISPLACEMENT

TRAIT

INTERVIEW

PROJECTIVE TECHNIQUE

THEMATIC APPERCEPTION TEST (TAT)

PERSONALITY

LIFE INSTINCTS (EROS)

ID

EGO

SUPEREGO

DEFENSE MECHANISMS

DENIAL

FANTASY

REGRESSION

NEO-FREUDIANS

BEHAVIORAL OBSERVATION

MMPI

RORSCHACH INK BLOT TEST

MATCHING TOPICS 10A, B

Match the following key terms with the appropriate definition.

_____ 1. MMPI

_____ 3. repression

_____ 5. death instincts

_____ 7. projective technique

_____ 9. behavioral observation

_____ 11. fantasy

_____ 13. life instincts

_____ 15. interview

_____ 17. idealistic principle

_____ 19. id

_____ 21. pleasure principle

_____ 23. denial

_____ 25. trait

_____ 27. rationalization

_____ 2. psychoanalytic approach

_____ 4. neo-Freudians

_____ 6. theory

_____ 8. superego

_____ 10. projection

_____ 12. regression

_____ 14. ego

_____ 16. Rorschach Ink Blot Test

_____ 18. personality

_____ 20. reality principle

_____ 22. defense mechanisms

_____ 24. Thematic Apperception Test

_____ 26. displacement

a. The approach to personality associated with Freud and his followers that relies on instincts and the unconscious as explanatory concepts.

b. Personality theorists (including Adler, Jung, and Horney) that kept many basic psychoanalytic principles, but differed from a strict Freudian view, adding new concepts of their own.

c. Inborn impulses proposed by Freud that compel one toward survival, including hunger, thirst, and sex.

d. A personality assessment technique requiring a subject to respond to ambiguous stimuli, thus projecting his or her self into the responses.

e. Inborn impulses proposed by Freud that compel one toward destruction, including aggression and hostility.

f. The instinctive aspect of personality that seeks immediate gratification of impulses; operates on the pleasure principle.

g. The impulse of the id to seek immediate gratification to reduce tensions.

h. The aspect of personality that encompasses the sense of "self"; in contact with the real world; operates on the reality principle.

i. Force that governs the ego; arbitrating between the demands of the id, the superego, and the real world.

j. Unconsciously applied techniques that protect the self (ego) from feelings of anxiety.

k. The aspect of personality that refers to ethical or moral considerations; operates on the idealistic principle.

l. The force that governs the superego; opposed to the id, seeks adherence to standards of ethics and morality.

m. A projective personality test requiring a subject to tell a series of short stories about a set of ambiguous pictures.

n. A return to earlier, childish levels of previously reinforcing behaviors as an escape from anxiety-producing situations.

o. Any distinguishable, relatively enduring way in which one individual differs from others.

p. Seeing in others those very characteristics and motives that cause stress in one's self.

q. The personality assessment technique of drawing conclusions about one's personality based on observations of one's behaviors.

r. The personality assessment technique involving a conversational interchange between the interviewer and subject to gain information about the subject.

s. A paper-and-pencil inventory of 567 true-false questions used to assess a number of personality dimensions, some of which may indicate the presence of a psychological disorder.

t. A personality assessment technique requiring subjects to respond to ambiguous stimuli, thus projecting his or her "self" into their responses.

u. A projective technique in which the subject is asked to say what he or she sees in a series of ink blots.

v. An escape from stress through imagination and daydreaming.

w. Generating excuses to explain one's behaviors rather than facing the real (anxiety-producing) reasons for those behaviors.

x. An organized collection of ultimately testable ideas used to explain a particular subject matter.

y. Those affects, cognitions, and behaviors that can be said to characterize an individual in several situations, and over time.

z. "Motivated forgetting" in which stressful, potentially anxiety-producing events are forced from awareness into the unconscious.

aa. Directing one's motives at some substitute person or object rather than expressing them directly.

TRUE-FALSE TEST TOPIC 10A

_____ 1. A major debate among psychologists is the extent to which personality is related to consistent behavior across different situations.

_____ 2. Current research suggests that personality traits are stable over a wide range of situations.

_____ 3. Reliance on innate drives and the influence of the unconscious characterize the humanistic theory of personality.

_____ 4. Aspects of one's mental life that are not presently conscious may be either preconscious or unconscious.

_____ 5. Freud was influenced by the writings of Descartes.

_____ 6. Freud referred to the energy for sexual instincts as Eros.

_____ 7. Whereas the id is believed to be inborn, the ego and superego develop.

_____ 8. Freud's defense mechanisms defend us against loss of self esteem.

_____ 9. Freud's theory of psychosexual development is based on the assumption that even infants and young children are influenced by sexual impulses.

_____ 10. Adler, Jung, and Horney were neo-Freudians.

_____ 11. A major criticism of psychoanalytic theory is that many of the ideas are untestable.

_____ 12. The behaviorists disagreed with the principles of psychoanalytic theory on the basis that the study of the unconscious was not observable or verifiable.

_____ 13. Albert Bandura is a neo-Freudian who suggested that personality is learned by observing the behaviors of others and noting which of those behaviors are reinforced.

_____ 14. The humanistic-phenomenological approach to personality suggests that what matters most is how a person views himself and other people.

_____ 15. Abraham Maslow criticized most of the current psychological theory of his time as being too negative and pessimistic.

_____ 16. Allport and Cattell have in common the fact that they are trait theorists.

_____ 17. Cattell used a statistical technique called analysis of variance to identify underlying personality traits.

_____ 18. The Five-Factor Model is a substitute for the lack of agreement among psychologists regarding any basic personality traits.

_____ 19. Collectivist cultures are more interested in personality traits than individualist cultures.

_____ 20. One disadvantage of trait theories is that they offer little more than just description.

TRUE-FALSE TEST TOPIC 10B

_____ 1. Behavioral observations may be particularly useful if the observations are purposeful, careful, and structured.

_____ 2. One advantage of assessing personality by interview is flexibility.

_____ 3. The MMPI is the most researched test in all of psychology.

_____ 4. The MMPI and the Rorschach are the same type of personality tests.

_____ 5. Both the MMPI and the CPI are multiphasic tests.

_____ 6. On a projective test, subjects' answers are considered either right or wrong.

_____ 7. A simple word association test could be considered a projective technique.

_____ 8. The TAT is the best known of the projective tests.

FILL-IN TEST TOPIC 10A

1. A _____ is an organized collection of testable ideas used to explain a particular subject matter.

2. _____ was among the first psychologists to question the concept of consistency of personality.

3. Freud's technique of therapy that was derived from his personality theory is known as _____.

4. Freud referred to the life instincts as _____.

5. The impulses of destruction are referred to as death instincts or _____.

6. A five year old begins to suck her thumb again and cling to her mother when her new baby brother arrives home from the hospital. Freud would call her behavior _____.

7. When he learned of his father's diagnosis of cancer, Fred simply could not believe it was true. He was employing the Freudian defense mechanism called _____.

8. The Oedipus and Electra complexes occur during the _____ stage of psychosexual development.

9. The psychologist chosen by Freud to be his successor, and the man who developed the idea of the collective unconscious was _____ _____.

10. Carl Jung believed that the unconscious contained universal patterns and forms called _____.

11. The neo-Freudian who developed the notion of the inferiority complex was _____.

12. Dollard and Miller argued that personality is determined by one's _____ which are formed in response to environmental cues.

13. _____ suggested that humans have a basic goal to become fully functioning.

14. A distinguishable, relatively enduring way in which one individual differs from another is a/an _____.

15. Gordon Allport described characteristics that are shared by almost everyone as _____ traits.

FILL-IN TEST TOPIC 10B

1. The _____ is the most important instrument of clinical assessment.
2. Using a technique called _____, a psychologist may have a client act out a given life situation in order to learn more about the client's personality.
3. The MMPI is called _____ because it measures several different personality dimensions with the same items.
4. The 16 PF Questionnaire was developed by _____.
5. The Rorschach and the TAT are _____ tests.

MULTIPLE CHOICE TEST TOPIC 10A

1. One of the big debates among personality psychologists has been the extent to which one's personality leads one to behave
   a. criminally.
   b. consistently.
   c. maturely.
   d. appropriately.

2. Which of the following was not a source for Freud's personality theory?
   a. observation of his patients
   b. self-examination
   c. collaboration with other psychologists
   d. reading the works of philosophers

3. At times, Patty contemplates suicide. Which of the following terms would best describe in Freudian terms what motivates those thoughts?
   a. basic instincts
   b. the preconscious
   c. Eros
   d. Thanatos

4. The Freudian personality structure that is considered to be innate is the
   a. id.
   b. ego.
   c. superego.
   d. libido.

5. Freud proposed that defense mechanisms develop unconsciously to help us cope with
   a. depression.
   b. thoughts of suicide.
   c. biological drives.
   d. anxiety.

6. Directing one's motives at some substitute person or object rather than expressing it directly is a defense mechanism referred to as
   a. repression.
   b. projection.
   c. displacement.
   d. fantasy.

7. Sammy's parents refuse to believe that he has cancer and continue to tell their friends that he has had surgery to remove a "cyst." They are practicing the defense mechanism of
   a. denial.
   b. displacement.
   c. fantasy
   d. rationalization.

8. Jayna tells her mother that she will never kiss a yucky boy. She is probably in the _____ stage of psychosexual development.
   a. oral
   b. anal
   c. phallic
   d. latency

9. Billy is almost three years old, and insists that he must "go to the potty" every time the family gets in the car to go for an outing. Billy is likely in the _____ stage of psychosexual development.
   a. oral
   b. anal
   c. phallic
   d. genital

10. Freud's notion of penis envy occurred during the _____ stage of psychosexual development.
   a. oral
   b. anal
   c. phallic
   d. latency

11. Alfred Adler developed the idea of the
   a. inferiority complex.
   b. defense mechanism.
   c. collective unconscious.
   d. phenomenological approach.

12. The neo-Freudian who theorized that people have three ways of interacting—moving away, moving toward, and moving against other people—was
   a. Alfred Adler.
   b. Carl Jung.
   c. Karen Horney.
   d. Anna Freud.

13. Alfred Adler, Carl Jung, and Karen Horney all have in common the fact that they
   a. had their beginnings in the psychoanalytic theory.
   b. were neo-Freudians.
   c. offered alternate ideas to psychoanalytic theory.
   d. all of the above.

14. Which of the following is a criticism of Freud's psychoanalytic theory of personality?
   a. It is not a comprehensive view of the phenomenon of personality.
   b. Many of the ideas are not testable.
   c. The theory is too simplistic.
   d. The theory focuses too much on adult development.

15. Which of the following may be viewed as the major advantage of the so-called behavioral-learning approach to personality?
   a. Most of the psychologists who support this approach were already famous for other contributions.
   b. It focuses entirely on external forces, such as the environment and other people.
   c. It relies on concepts that are observable and measurable.
   d. It has given rise to the fullest, most comprehensive of theories.

16. Which of the following is NOT a behaviorist?
    a. Skinner
    b. Maslow
    c. Watson
    d. Dollard

17. Watson and his followers emphasized the role of _____ in the determination of one's behaviors.
    a. personality
    b. environment
    c. heredity
    d. motivation

18. Skinnerians argue that behavior is shaped by
    a. consequences.
    b. heredity.
    c. habits.
    d. modeling.

19. Albert Bandura differs from other behavioral-learning theorists in that he is
    a. focused on the effects of consequences on behavior.
    b. interested in the role of habits in influencing personality.
    c. willing to consider the internal, cognitive processes of the learner.
    d. uninterested in how behavior is learned.

20. Which of the following is NOT a criticism of the behavioral-learning approach?
    a. The behavioral-learning approach dehumanizes personality.
    b. The behavioral-learning approach is too deterministic.
    c. The behavioral-learning approach has considerable application in behavior therapy.
    d. None of the above.

21. Which of the following theories places the least emphasis on the role of the environment in shaping personality?
    a. behavioral-learning approach
    b. psychoanalytic theory
    c. observational learning
    d. humanistic-phenomenological approach

22. A particular strength of the humanistic-phenomenological approach is its emphasis on
    a. the past.
    b. the role of the environment.
    c. the positive notion of personal growth and development.
    d. measurable and observable phenomena.

23. Which of the following personality theories was criticized for relying too heavily on the notion of biological drives and concepts that are untestable?
    a. psychoanalytic approach
    b. trait theory
    c. behaviorist approach
    d. humanism

24. A distinction of trait theories is that they focus more on
    a. the influence of heredity.
    b. explaining personality.
    c. describing personality.
    d. refuting the influence of environmental factors.

25. Which of the following is NOT a correct match?
    a. Allport - cardinal traits
    b. Allport - surface traits
    c. Cattell - factor analysis
    d. Cattell - source traits

26. Which of the following is NOT one of the "Big Five" dimensions of personality in the recently developed "Five-Factor Model"?
    a. extroversion-introversion
    b. agreeableness
    c. conscientiousness
    d. stability-instability

MULTIPLE CHOICE TEST TOPIC 10B

1. Which of the following would be the LEAST valid reason for personality assessment?
   a. theory construction
   b. genetic planning
   c. predicting other behaviors
   d. clinical diagnosis

2. If you meet someone new at a party, what personality assessment technique are you likely to use to evaluate that person?
   a. interview
   b. paper and pencil test
   c. behavioral observation
   d. both a and c

3. Which of the following techniques may be used to supplement behavioral observation?
   a. projective tests
   b. role playing and rating scales
   c. interviews
   d. paper and pencil tests

4. When analyzing responses to the TAT, what does a psychologist look for?
   a. emerging themes or stories that provide insights about the subject
   b. the extent to which the subject attended to or ignored the colors in the stimulus card
   c. the average number of items correct for each subtest
   d. attention to detail and descriptions of animals

5. In what way is the MMPI a "criterion referenced" test?
   a. Items were included only if they differentiated among diagnosed groups.
   b. The standardization groups, used to establish test norms, were very large.
   c. The test includes items that determine the extent to which the subject is taking the test seriously.
   d. The authors had a full and complete theory of personality traits in mind before they began writing test items.

6. Which of the following is the most commonly used personality inventory?
   a. the California Personality Inventory
   b. the 16 PF
   c. the MMPI
   d. the TAT

7. Which of the following personality inventories is NOT multiphasic?
   a. the Taylor Manifest Anxiety Scale
   b. the 16 PF
   c. the MMPI
   d. the California Personality Inventory

8. One hallmark of projective tests is that they
   a. are multiphasic.
   b. are criterion-referenced.
   c. require responses to ambiguous stimuli.
   d. measure only one trait.

9. Which of the following is NOT a projective technique?
   a. word association
   b. MMPI
   c. Rorschach
   d. Rotter Incomplete Sentences Blank

10. The TAT was originally designed to measure
    a. depression.
    b. personality disorders.
    c. personality traits.
    d. achievement motivation.

ESSENTIAL STRATEGIES FOR SUCCESS #10

SUGGESTIONS FOR TAKING NOTES

1. At the start of class, date your notes and give them a title that corresponds with the chapter to be presented in lecture. Be sure to number the pages as you go and date each page.

2. Don't try to write every word the professor says, just get the important facts and details. Listen for key words that alert you to what's coming. Numerical terms signal a list, e.g., "three" reasons for taking good notes are... Other possible key words and phrases are "if," "then," "when," "next," "as a result," "leading up to," "because of." I am sure you get the idea.

3. If the professor writes something on the board or an overhead projector, write it down.

4. Write your notes in your own words. It is important that you understand what you write and not just memorize words that have no real meaning for you.

5. Try to write in complete thoughts or sentences as much as possible.

6. Ask your instructor to clarify any points you don't understand.

7. Review your notes as soon after class as possible, definitely the same day. The longer you wait, the more difficult it will be to add any ideas, clarify, or rewrite.

8. Use your textbook or handouts to add or clarify points you don't understand.

9. Use abbreviations only to the extent that you can understand or remember the symbols and short forms you are using and interpret them later.

10. Do not rely solely on your notes for studying. You must also read your text and other assigned material.

CHAPTER 11 PSYCHOLOGY, STRESS, AND PHYSICAL HEALTH

LEARNING OBJECTIVES

The following items represent the fundamental concepts that you should know when you have finished studying this chapter. Read them now as a chapter preview and return to them to test your knowledge after you have studied.

Topic A
1. Define stress and stressors.
2. Define environmental and personal frustration, and give an example of each.
3. Name four types of motivational conflict and give an example of each.
4. Discuss the SRRS as a measure of life-induced stress.
5. Discuss the role of SES in stress.
6. Describe the Lazarus' theory of life-induced stress.
7. Describe the general adaptation syndrome.
8. Discuss effective and ineffective strategies for coping with stress.
9. Explain the frustration-aggression hypothesis.

Topic B
1. List four assumptions that form the basis of the involvement of psychologists in the realm of physical health.
2. Describe the Type A behavior pattern and discuss its relationship to health.
3. Discuss the potential role of psychology in helping people to stop smoking.
4. List eight strategies used by health psychologists to help patients follow doctor's orders.
5. Discuss how psychologists can have an impact on the spread of AIDS.

VOCABULARY CHAPTER 11

On your own paper, write the definition for each of the following key terms. Your learning will be facilitated by writing the definition in your own words rather than copying the exact definition from your text.

GENERAL ADAPTATION SYNDROME (GAS)   STRESS
STRESSORS   FRUSTRATION
HEALTH PSYCHOLOGY   TYPE A BEHAVIOR PATTERN
CONFLICT   ANXIETY
FRUSTRATION-AGGRESSION HYPOTHESIS   SOCIOECONOMIC STATUS (SES)

MATCHING TOPIC 11A, B

Match the following key terms from your textbook with the appropriate definition.

_____ 1. frustration-aggression hypothesis	_____ 2. frustration
_____ 3. Type A behavior pattern	_____ 4. stress
_____ 5. conflict	_____ 6. stressors
_____ 7. anxiety	_____ 8. general adaptation syndrome
_____ 9. health psychology	_____ 10. socioeconomic status

a. A collection of behaviors (competitive, achievement oriented, impatient, easily aroused, often hostile or angry) often associated with coronary heart disease.

b. A complex pattern of reactions to real or perceived threats to one's sense of well-being that motivates adjustment.

c. Real or perceived threats to one's sense of well-being; sources of stress.

d. A stressor; the blocking or thwarting of goal-directed behavior.

e. A stressor in which some goals can be satisfied only at the expense of others.

f. A general feeling of tension, apprehension, or dread that involves predictable physiological changes.

g. The view (now discredited) that all aggression stems from frustration.

h. The field of applied psychology that studies psychological factors affecting physical health and illness.

i. A pattern of physiological reactions to stressors including alarm, resistance, and exhaustion.

j. A measure that reflects one's income, educational level, and occupation.

TRUE-FALSE TEST TOPIC 11A

_____ 1. People typically feel stress when their sense of well being is threatened.

_____ 2. Stress that results from frustration represents a normal reaction.

_____ 3. Environmental frustration implies that goal-directed behavior is being blocked by something or someone in the environment.

_____ 4. Approach-approach conflicts do not produce stress since both alternatives are desirable.

_____ 5. Avoidance-avoidance conflicts are the most stress producing of all conflicts.

_____ 6. The Social Readjustment Rating Scale was developed by Richard Lazarus.

_____ 7. The positive correlation between scores on the SRRS and physical illness indicates that stress causes illness.

_____ 8. People of high socioeconomic status are less likely than people of low socioeconomic status to experience stress.

_____ 9. Holmes and Rahe argue that the big life changes are more stressful, whereas Lazarus argues that life's little hassles cause more stress.

_____ 10. Challenge, control, and commitment are factors that seem related to how a person handles stress.

_____ 11. The general adaptation syndrome describes the psychological reactions to stress.

_____ 12. Alarm, reaction, and resistance are the three stages of the general adaptation syndrome.

_____ 13. Physical exercise is good for our health, but has no value as a stress reliever.

_____ 14. Psychologists widely accept the notion that frustration is the single known source of aggression.

_____ 15. Stress is often accompanied by anxiety.

TRUE-FALSE TEST TOPIC 11B

_____ 1. The involvement of psychologists in the medical realm of physical health is in part based on the assumption that certain behaviors are related to disease.

_____ 2. There is evidence that personality characteristics and physical health are correlated.

_____ 3. Logan Wright suggests that time urgency, chronic activation, and multiphasia are the key components of Type A behavior pattern related to coronary heart disease.

_____ 4. After one heart attack, women with Type A behavior are still more likely to have another heart attack than their Type B counterparts.

_____ 5. One role of the health psychologist is to bring about changes in potentially dangerous or unhealthy behaviors.

_____ 6. Health psychologists can do little to promote healthy behaviors, and must be content to work on reducing harmful behaviors.

_____ 7. Virtually all individuals who develop full-blown AIDS will die within four years.

_____ 8. Small group sessions presenting information and providing support have been effective in changing sexual behaviors in high risk populations.

FILL-IN TEST TOPIC 11A, B

1. The stimuli for stress are called _____.

2. The blocking of goal-directed behavior results in _____.

3. A choice between two equally desirable goals is called a/an _____ conflict.

4. The most stressful type of conflict is the _____.

5. The Social Rating Readjustment Scale measures stress brought about by _____.

6. Richard Lazarus argued that stress doesn't result from the big life changes, but more from the everyday little events or _____.

7. The SRRS was developed by _____ and Rahe.

8. In the context of stress reduction, _____ _____ refers to a re-thinking of the nature of the situation so as to cast it in the best possible light.

9. A general feeling of tension, apprehension, and dread, that involves predictable physiological changes refers to _____.

10. At one time, _____ was believed to be the only cause of aggression.

11. _____ behavior pattern is associated with coronary heart disease.

12. The stages of the general adaptation syndrome are alarm, resistance, and
    _____.

13. The tendency to have a number of projects all going at once is called
    _____.

14. Health psychologists work toward the understanding, treatment, and
    _____ of disease.

15. _____ is the leading cause of premature death in the industrialized world.

16. Nearly _____ percent of those who quit smoking relapse within a year.

17. _____ is an STD with no cure and no effective treatment.

MULTIPLE CHOICE TEST TOPIC 11A

1. According to your text, which of the following is NOT considered one of the
   sources of stress?
   a. aggression
   b. frustration
   c. life events
   d. conflict

2. The relationship between environmental frustration and personal frustration may also
   be characterized as
   a. stimulus vs. response.
   b. need vs. drive.
   c. social vs. nonsocial.
   d. external vs. internal.

3. Nell wants to eat dessert every night, but she does not want to gain weight. She will
   probably experience the frustration of a/an _____ conflict.
   a. approach-approach
   b. avoidance-avoidance
   c. approach-avoidance
   d. multiple approach-avoidance

4. According to Richard Lazarus, which of the following events would be more stressful?
   a. retirement
   b. divorce
   c. moving to another city
   d. a series of small breakdowns that put your car in the shop

5. According to Holmes, which of the following events would be more stressful?
   a. getting stuck in a traffic jam
   b. divorce
   c. arguing with someone at work
   d. having your washing machine breakdown

6. Which of the following is NOT likely to reduce stress?
   a. relaxation
   b. exercise
   c. cognitive reappraisal
   d. focusing on a smaller hassle

7. Which of the following describes a conflict in which both alternatives are positive?
   a. approach-avoidance
   b. approach-approach
   c. avoidance-avoidance
   d. none of the above

8. Socioeconomic status (SES) is related to stress in that
   a. the higher the SES the higher the stress.
   b. the higher the SES the less ability to deal with stress.
   c. the lower the SES the fewer resources the person has for dealing with stress.
   d. the lower the SES the more "happy go lucky" the person is and the less he or she is bothered by stress.

9. Researchers have established that the Social Readjustment Rating Scale
   a. is unrelated to incidence of physical illness.
   b. is positively correlated to physical illness.
   c. predicts mental illness.
   d. none of the above.

10. According to Dollard's frustration-aggression hypothesis,
    a. frustration and aggression always go together.
    b. both frustration and aggression can be reduced by exercise.
    c. aggression may produce many different types of frustration.
    d. aggression is always caused by frustration.

11. Compared to the Social Readjustment Rating Scale, the Hassles Scale, developed by Richard Lazarus,
    a. predicts physical health and psychological symptoms even better.
    b. predicts nothing of any significance.
    c. predicts psychological symptoms but not physical health.
    d. is a worse predictor of physical health.

12. The type of conflict which creates the most stress is
    a. avoidance-avoidance.
    b. approach-approach.
    c. multiple approach-avoidance.
    d. approach-avoidance.

13. Jess wants to play basketball for the University of Houston Cougars when he grows up. However, current predictions of his height indicate that he will be only about five feet eight inches tall. This situation is an example of
    a. environmental frustration.
    b. personal frustration.
    c. approach-avoidance conflict.
    d. approach-approach conflict.

14. "Out of the frying pan and into the fire," is a cliché' which refers to a/an _____ conflict.
    a. avoidance-avoidance
    b. approach-approach
    c. multiple approach-avoidance
    d. approach-avoidance

15. In coping with stress, the opposite of change is
    a. stagnation.
    b. fixation.
    c. frustration.
    d. adaptation.

16. Which of the following reactions or responses to stress would be considered maladaptive?
    a. relaxation
    b. cognitive reappraisal
    c. aggression
    d. exercise

17. You are vulnerable to physical illness and infection to a greater degree than normal. Although the sympathetic response seems to have returned to normal, the physiological systems continue to mobilize bodily reserves. You are in the _____ stage of the general adaptation syndrome.
    a. alarm
    b. resistance
    c. fixation
    d. exhaustion

18. Which of the following psychologists first described the general adaptation syndrome?
    a. Holmes
    b. Lazarus
    c. Selye
    d. Meichenbaum

19. Which of the following responses is NOT likely to be the result of stress?
    a. aggression
    b. anxiety
    c. physical illness
    d. increased optimism

20. Which of the following characteristics is NOT descriptive of a "hardy" personality?
    a. control
    b. challenge
    c. carefree
    d. commitment

MULTIPLE CHOICE TEST TOPIC 11B

1. Which of the following is NOT an assumption for the basis of health psychology?
   a. Certain behaviors increase the risk of certain chronic diseases.
   b. You can change any behavior using humanistic principles.
   c. Changes in behaviors can reduce the risk of certain diseases.
   d. Behavioral interventions are comparatively cost-effective.

2. According to Logan Wright, which of the following is NOT a part of Type A behavior pattern associated with coronary heart disease?
   a. time urgency
   b. chronic activation
   c. multiphasia
   d. achievement-orientation

3. Which of the following statements regarding Type A behavior and coronary heart disease are TRUE?
   a. Women with Type A behavior are more likely to have heart attacks than women with Type B behavior.
   b. Type A and Type B persons show no difference in baseline measures of heart rate and blood pressure, but do show differences when under stress.
   c. Recent research suggests that personality and behavior patterns are not related to coronary heart diseases as was once believed.
   d. Type A and Type B individuals are easily distinguished with pencil and paper tests.

4. Which of the following is TRUE?
   a. About 400,000 deaths per year can be traced to tobacco use.
   b. Alcohol kills more people than tobacco.
   c. More people die from traffic accidents than from sexual behaviors.
   d. The leading cause of death among Americans aged 25-44 is traffic accidents.

5. One approach that seems to be effective in getting adolescents to refrain from smoking does so by emphasizing
   a. long-term benefits of not smoking.
   b. potential harm of lifelong smoking.
   c. short-term benefits of not smoking.
   d. scare tactics showing individuals with cancer.

ESSENTIAL STRATEGIES FOR SUCCESS #11

USING 3 X 5 CARDS

An excellent way to study the extensive vocabulary that psychology presents is to use 3 x 5 cards. Prepare the cards by writing the term you want to learn on one side and a definition or related fact on the other side. Take the cards with you in your purse or pocket and study them whenever you have a few minutes. You might be stuck in traffic or waiting in the dentist's office, or you might even get out of class a few minutes early. Remember, we have already discussed the benefits of short, frequent study periods.

Tape a few of the cards around your bathroom mirror and study them while you shave, brush your teeth, or comb your hair. You will be surprised how much you gain from these few minutes. Ten minutes a day for six days means one hour that you don't have to spend in the library or sitting at your desk.

When you study the cards, look at the term and say the definition aloud. If you can define the term, place the card in a discard pile. If you cannot, then read the definition three times and place the card on the bottom of the stack. When you have gone through the cards once, shuffle them just as you would playing cards. This prevents you from learning the definitions in some sort of order and becoming dependent on that order as a memory cue. A real benefit of this study method is that you have evidence that it works: just look at the discard pile. That represents the terms you have already learned. In addition, the studying task has been reduced. Each time you study, you are focusing on the information you do not know and you are reducing the learning task as you discard the terms you do know.

CHAPTER 12—THE PSYCHOLOGICAL DISORDERS

LEARNING OBJECTIVES

The following items represent the fundamental concepts that you should know when you have finished studying this chapter. Read them now as a chapter preview and return to them to test your knowledge after you have studied.

Topic A
1. Explain how psychological abnormality is defined.
2. Describe the DSM-IV and discuss the advantages of having a classification system for disorders.
3. Discuss problems associated with classification and labeling.
4. Define insanity and discuss the appropriate use of the term.

Topic B
1. Characterize the specific anxiety disorders, including etiology and prognosis when applicable.
2. Distinguish between obsessions and compulsions.
3. Distinguish between hypochondriasis and conversion disorder.
4. Describe three dissociative disorders.
5. Characterize personality disorders.
6. Discuss the cognitive disorders and particularly Alzheimer's diseases.
7. Define mood disorders and discuss their prevalence and causes.
8. Discuss the major symptoms of schizophrenia and identify the DSM subtypes.
9. Distinguish between process and reactive schizophrenia.
10. Distinguish between positive and negative symptoms of schizophrenia.
11. Describe the factors suspected as causes of schizophrenia.
12. Discuss the special problem of attention-deficit/hyperactivity disorder.

VOCABULARY CHAPTER 12

On your own paper, write the definition for each of the following key terms. Your learning will be facilitated by writing the definition in your own words rather than copying the exact definition from your text.

ABNORMAL
ETIOLOGY
ANXIETY
PROGNOSIS
PANIC DISORDER
DSM-IV
OBSESSIVE-COMPULSIVE DISORDER
OBSESSIONS
SOMATOFORM DISORDERS
CONVERSION DISORDER
DISSOCIATIVE AMNESIA
DISSOCIATIVE IDENTITY DISORDER
DELIRIUM
AMNESTIC DISORDERS
DYSTHYMIA
MANIA
MOOD DISORDERS
PROCESS SCHIZOPHRENIA
HALLUCINATIONS

DIAGNOSIS
INSANITY
PHOBIC DISORDER
AGORAPHOBIA
GENERALIZED ANXIETY DISORDER
COMORBIDITY
COMPULSIONS
POSTRAUMATIC STRESS DISORDER
HYPOCHONDRIASIS
DISSOCIATIVE DISORDERS
DISSOCIATIVE FUGUE
PERSONALITY DISORDERS
DEMENTIA
MAJOR DEPRESSION
BIPOLAR DISORDER
REACTIVE SCHIZOPHRENIA
SCHIZOPHRENIA
DELUSIONS
DOPAMINE HYPOTHESIS

MATCHING TOPIC 12A

Match the following key terms from your textbook with the appropriate definition.

_____ 1. compulsions
_____ 3. comorbidity
_____ 5. diagnosis
_____ 7. posttraumatic stress disorder
_____ 9. prognosis
_____ 11. conversion disorder
_____ 13. obsessive-compulsive disorder
_____ 15. panic disorder
_____ 17. DSM-IV

_____ 2. dissociative disorders
_____ 4. somatoform disorders
_____ 6. hypochondriasis
_____ 8. obsessions
_____ 10. etiology
_____ 12. abnormal
_____ 14. insanity
_____ 16. agoraphobia
_____ 18. generalized anxiety disorder

_____ 19. phobic disorder   _____ 20. anxiety

a. Maladaptive cognitions, affect, and/or behaviors that are at odds with social or cultural expectations and that result in distress or discomfort.
b. The act of recognizing a disorder on the basis of the presence of particular symptoms.
c. Ideas or thoughts that involuntarily and persistently intrude into awareness.
d. Disorders in which the person tries in some way to flee or escape from an aspect of personality or experience that is the source of distress.
e. A general feeling of apprehension or dread accompanied by predictable physiological changes.
f. An intense, irrational fear that leads a person to avoid the feared object, activity, or situation.
g. An anxiety disorder in which disruptive recollections, distressing dreams, flashbacks, and felt anxiety occur well after the experience of a traumatic event.
h. A phobic fear of open places, of being alone, or of being in public places from which escape might be difficult.
i. A disorder in which anxiety attacks occur suddenly and unpredictably; there may be periods free from anxiety.
j. Persistent, chronic, and distressingly high levels of unattributable anxiety.
k. An anxiety disorder characterized by a pattern of recurrent obsessions and compulsions.
l. Constantly intruding, stereotyped, and essentially involuntary acts or behaviors.
m. Psychological disorders that reflect imagined physical or bodily symptoms or complaints.
n. A mental disorder involving the unrealistic fear of developing some serious disease or illness.
o. The display of a severe physical disorder for which there is no medical explanation; often accompanied by an apparent lack of concern on the part of the patient.
p. A publication of the American Psychiatric Association that lists, organizes, and describes psychological disorders.
q. The prediction of the future course of an illness or disorder.
r. The extent to which persons evidence symptoms of two or more disorders at the same time.
s. The source of cause, in this context, of psychological disorders.
t. A legal term involving judgments of diminished capacity and the inability to tell right from wrong.

MATCHING TOPIC 12B

Match the following key terms from your textbook with the appropriate definition.

_____ 1. dissociative amnesia   _____ 2. dissociative fugue
_____ 3. dissociative identity disorder   _____ 4. personality disorders
_____ 5. delirium   _____ 6. dementia
_____ 7. amnestic disorders   _____ 8. mood disorders
_____ 9. major depression   _____ 10. dysthymia
_____ 11. bipolar disorder   _____ 12. mania
_____ 13. schizophrenia   _____ 14. delusions
_____ 15. hallucinations   _____ 16. process schizophrenia
_____ 17. reactive schizophrenia   _____ 18. dopamine hypothesis

a. A loss of intellectual abilities; memory is poor and deteriorates; impulse control and judgment adversely affected.

b. The point of view that schizophrenia results from unusually high levels of the neurotransmitter dopamine in the brain.

c. An extreme of mood characterized by intense sadness, feelings of hopelessness, and a loss of pleasure and interest in normal activities.

d. Complex psychotic disorders characterized by impairment of cognitive functioning, delusions and hallucinations, social withdrawal, and inappropriate affect.

e. A psychologically caused inability to recall important personal information.

f. Schizophrenia in which the onset of the symptoms is comparatively slow and gradual.

g. The existence within one individual of two or more personalities, each of which is dominant at a particular time.

h. Showing an impairment of memory while other cognitive functions remain intact.

i. An extreme of mood characterized by euphoria, a sense of well-being, and an increase in activity level.

j. A condition of amnesia accompanied by unexplained travel or change of location.

k. Schizophrenia in which the onset of symptoms is comparatively slow and gradual.

l. Enduring patterns of perceiving, relating to, and thinking about the environment and one's self that are inflexible and maladaptive.

m. Disorders of affect or feeling; usually depression; less frequently mania and depression occurring in cycles.

n. A severe mood disorder evidenced by unexplainable swings of mood between the more common depression and mania.

o. A clouded state of consciousness with a lessening of cognitive awareness and attention.

p. False beliefs; ideas that are firmly held regardless of what others say or do.

q. A reasonably mild, though chronic disorder of depression associated with low energy and low self-esteem.

r. False perceptions; perceiving that which is not there.

TRUE-FALSE TEST TOPIC 12A, B

_____ 1. Abnormality implies that behaviors or mental processes are maladaptive, statistically rare, culturally inappropriate, and cause distress or discomfort.

_____ 2. The DSM-IV is a publication of the American Psychological Association.

_____ 3. The etiology of a disorder refers to the recovery rate of patients who have the disorder.

_____ 4. A major advantage of the DSM-IV classification system is that it facilitates communication among professionals.

_____ 5. One problem with labeling disorders is that labels can create lasting stigmas and negative attitudes about people.

_____ 6. Insanity is a legal term and not a psychological term.

_____ 7. Anxiety based disorders are more common in men than in women.

_____ 8. Individuals who suffer from generalized anxiety disorder may be likely to abuse drugs and alcohol.

_____ 9. Panic disorder is characterized more by chronic anxiety than by acute anxiety.

_____ 10. The prognosis is good for phobic disorders.

_____ 11. Grooming behaviors and checking behaviors are common compulsions.

_____ 12. The comorbidity associated with PTSD may take the form of drug or alcohol abuse or depression.

_____ 13. A person who experiences conversion disorder is called a hypochondriac.

_____ 14. One difference between hypochondriasis and conversion disorder is that in conversion disorder, there is a real medical problem.

_____ 15. In dissociative amnesia, the person usually forgets the trauma that leads up to the amnesia.

_____ 16. Multiple personality or dissociative identity disorder is not the same disorder as schizophrenia.

_____ 17. Personality disorders are diagnosed when maladaptive behaviors have been long-standing, usually since childhood or adolescence.

_____ 18. Delirium and dementia are just two names for the same dysfunctional symptoms.

_____ 19. The early stages of Alzheimer's disease are marked by loss of long-term memory.

_____ 20. Major depression is twice as common in women as in men.

_____ 21. There is good evidence of a genetic predisposition for bipolar mood disorder.

_____ 22. Schizophrenic individuals rarely suffer from both delusions and hallucinations.

_____ 23. Although schizophrenics usually lose touch with reality, their affect is generally appropriate.

_____ 24. Actually, schizophrenia is a label that refers to many different disorders.

_____ 25. Although the relative attention to the disorders makes them seem like new phenomena, attention deficit/hyperactive disorders were actually first described in the late 1800s.

FILL-IN TEST TOPIC 12A, B

1. The _____ is the most widely used classification system in all of mental health.

2. The legal term for mental disorders which is not used in psychology is _____.

3. _____ refers to having two or more diseases or illnesses at the same time.

4. Phobic disorders are characterized by persistent _____.

5. Fear of open places is known as _____.

6. Hand washing, grooming, counting and checking behaviors are common _____.

7. Victims of kidnapping or rape are likely to suffer from _____ _____ disorder.

8. The _____ disorders involve physical or bodily complaints and symptoms.

9. A person preoccupied with the fear of developing or having some serious disease is suffering from _____.

10. _____ _____ is the illness that led Freud to develop psychoanalysis.

11. When a person suffering from amnesia finds himself in a different location, it is referred to as _____ _____.

12. _____ personality disorder is characterized by extreme sensitivity, suspiciousness, envy, and mistrust of others.

13. A person who is overly dramatic, reactive, and displays intensely expressed behaviors is suffering from _____ personality disorder.

14. _____ is a clouded state of consciousness, involving lessening of awareness and difficulty paying attention.

15. The most common type of amnestic disorder is dementia of the _____ type.

16. What were once described as affective disorders, are now referred to as _____ disorders.

17. The opposite of depression is _____.

18. People who swing back and forth between depression and mania, with interspersed periods of normal affect, are said to have _____ _____.

19. The most devastating, puzzling, and frustrating of all mental illnesses is _____.

20. _____ type schizophrenia is characterized by alternating periods of extreme withdrawal and extreme excitement.

21. Schizophrenic symptoms that have developed gradually over a period of years are referred to as _____ schizophrenia.

22. _____ schizophrenia refers to the sudden onset of schizophrenic symptoms.

23. One hypothesis about the cause of schizophrenia has to do with the presence of an abundance of the neurotransmitter, _____, in the brain.

24. The type of schizophrenia characterized by absurd, illogical, and changeable delusions and hallucinations is the _____ type.

25. _____ is a common stimulant used to treat attention deficit/hyperactive disorder.

MULTIPLE CHOICE TEST TOPIC 12A, B

1. Which of the following is NOT a criteria for determining abnormality in affect, behavior, or cognitions?
   a. maladaptive
   b. statistically common
   c. cause distress or discomfort
   d. culturally or socially inappropriate

2. When Kraepelin published the first classification scheme for mental disturbances, the cause of mental illness was thought to be
   a. biological.
   b. sociological.
   c. environmental.
   d. hereditary.

3. Which of the following is NOT one of the disadvantages or problems associated with classifying mental disorders?
   a. Classification explains the disorders, but does not offer treatment suggestions.
   b. Labeling people is dehumanizing.
   c. All the attention is focused on the individual and none on the family or society.
   d. Labels create lasting stigmas and negative attitudes about people.

4. Which of the following is a legal rather than a psychological term?
   a. diagnosis
   b. etiology
   c. insanity
   d. posttraumatic stress disorder

5. For which of the following phobias is a person most likely to seek treatment?
   a. fear of diseases
   b. fear of spiders
   c. fear of heights
   d. fear of open places

6. Charlotte has sudden, unpredictable, unprovoked attacks of intense anxiety. She is most likely suffering from
   a. panic disorder.
   b. agoraphobia.
   c. hypochondriasis.
   d. generalized anxiety disorder.

7. The difference between compulsive behavior such as gambling or eating, and the compulsions associated with OCD is that
   a. compulsive gamblers' feel more anxiety.
   b. the individual has more ability to control or decrease eating or gambling behavior.
   c. the compulsive gambler or eater experiences pleasure associated with the compulsive behavior.
   d. the compulsive eater or gambler feels more intense guilt about the behavior.

8. In posttraumatic stress disorder, the likelihood of recovery is related to the extent to which
   a. there are complicating factors such as alcoholism.
   b. the patient experienced psychological problems before the event.
   c. social support is available.
   d. all of the above.

9. La belle indifference is a secondary symptom occurring in association with
   a. somatoform disorders.
   b. conversion disorder.
   c. posttraumatic stress disorder.
   d. panic disorder.

10. The underlying theme of dissociative disorders is
   a. escape from an aspect of life that causes distress or anxiety.
   b. a break from reality.
   c. irrational fears that cause intense anxiety.
   d. mood swings that create abnormal affective responses.

11. Although it is not the same thing at all, the media often confuses dissociative personality disorder with
   a. hypochondriasis.
   b. amnesia.
   c. schizophrenia.
   d. agoraphobia.

12. One plausible explanation for psychogenic fugue and psychogenic amnesia is that they are
   a. an attempt to avoid stress.
   b. an attempt to get attention.
   c. a way of dealing with anxiety.
   d. a means of avoiding responsibility.

13. Unusually high incidences of child abuse, sexual abuse and drug abuse are related to
    a. schizophrenia.
    b. obsessive-compulsive disorder.
    c. dissociative identity disorder.
    d. dissociative fugue.

14. Personality disorders can be distinguished from other disorders on many grounds, but which of the following enables us to differentiate personality disorders from anxiety-based disorders? As opposed to anxiety-based disorders, personality disorders
    a. are more commonly a reaction to frustration and stress.
    b. involve a long-standing history of symptoms.
    c. are usually identified by adolescence.
    d. involve some degree of loss of contact with reality.

15. David seems to overreact to everything and constantly seeks attention and approval. At a party, he is the first to put a lamp shade on his head. He describes all his experiences as "peak, the best" and all his troubles as "the worst." He is most likely suffering from _____ personality disorder.
    a. passive-aggressive
    b. schizoid
    c. histrionic
    d. antisocial

16. Marge refuses to leave her husband or to file charges against him even though he has beaten her numerous times. She persists in believing that she is responsible for the abuse and that it will end if she figures out how to please him. She is most likely suffering from _____ personality disorder.
    a. dependent
    b. avoidant
    c. paranoid
    d. antisocial

17. Which of the following statements regarding Alzheimer's disease is NOT true?
    a. The early stages are marked by loss of short-term memory function.
    b. It is inevitable that individuals will experience Alzheimer's as they age.
    c. Three to four million Americans are afflicted with Alzheimer's dementia.
    d. Alzheimer's is a physical disease caused by changes in brain tissue.

18. Psychiatrist Aaron Beck offers an explanation for mood disorders that is largely
    a. behaviorist.
    b. cognitive.
    c. biological.
    d. situational.

19. Which of the following statements concerning schizophrenic patients is TRUE?
    a. They are usually colorless, socially withdrawn, and not at all dangerous.
    b. They usually exhibit wild, crazed behavior, and may be violent.
    c. Even though they may be having delusions, they are usually able to communicate clearly.
    d. The most common affect is extreme moods, either mania or depression.

20. Factors such as an excess of dopamine, normal brain configuration, severe disruptions early in family life and a relatively good response to treatment are correlated to _____ schizophrenia.
    a. reactive
    b. process
    c. positive
    d. negative

21. Everything else being equal, which person will have the greatest chance of being diagnosed with schizophrenia?
    a. Someone who knows and interacts with many schizophrenics on a regular basis.
    b. Someone who has an identical twin diagnosed as having the disorder.
    c. Someone with abnormally large ventricles in their cerebral cortex.
    d. Someone whose mother is generally cold, aloof, and unaffectionate.

22. The _____ type of schizophrenia is characterized by absurd, illogical, and changeable delusions, often accompanied by hallucinations resulting in severe impairment of judgment.
    a. undifferentiated
    b. residual
    c. catatonic
    d. paranoid

157

23. The _____ type of schizophrenia usually involves the most severe disintegration of personality.
    a. catatonic
    b. paranoid
    c. disorganized
    d. undifferentiated

24. _____ is the neurotransmitter associated with schizophrenia.
    a. Dopamine
    b. Acetylcholine
    c. Epinehprine
    d. Amphetamine

25. The rate of occurrence of attention deficit/hyperactive disorder in school children is estimated as high as ____ percent.
    a. 3
    b. 10
    c. 12
    d. 14

ESSENTIAL STRATEGIES FOR SUCCESS #12

TAKING ESSAY EXAMS

1. Read through the instructions to make sure you know how many questions to answer and what the scoring system will be. Plan which questions you will answer and in what order and budget your time for each question.

2. Organize and outline your answers to make sure you don't leave out any important information.

3. Read each question carefully and answer only what is asked. Look for key words: describe, define, list, explain, compare and contrast, illustrate.

4. Answer the questions that you know first. This will build your confidence.

5. Start your essay with a topic sentence, present the facts, and follow with a conclusion.

6. Use the vocabulary covered in class and in your text. Give specifics when possible.

7. Use examples to back up your judgments and opinions.

8. Leave space after each answer so you can go back and add details if you have extra time or remember additional facts.

9. Go back and reread each answer to be sure you didn't omit anything. Proofread for spelling and grammatical errors and correct them.

10. Prepare for the test by constructing your own essay questions and writing practice answers. The learning objectives in this study guide will be very helpful in anticipating essay questions.

****

Below are two essay questions that cover abnormal psychology. Use them to practice your essay writing techniques.

1. Discuss the advantages and disadvantages of diagnosis in abnormal psychology.
2. List and describe five subtypes of schizophrenia.

CHAPTER 13 — TREATMENT AND THERAPY

LEARNING OBJECTIVES

The following items represent the fundamental concepts that you should know when you have finished studying this chapter. Read them now as a chapter preview and return to them to test your knowledge after you have studied.

Topic A
1. Trace the history of the treatment of people with psychological disorders.
2. Describe the reform efforts of Phillipe Pinel, Benjamin Rush, Dorothea Dix, and Clifford Beers.
3. Differentiate among providers of treatment and therapy, according to credentials, work settings, and limitations on services provided.
4. Define prefrontal lobotomy and discuss its use both past and present.
5. Describe ECT and its current use.
6. Discuss treatment with antipsychotic drugs, listing the various drugs and their effects.
7. Discuss treatment with antidepressant drugs.
8. Discuss treatment with antianxiety drugs and the dangers of their use.

Topic B
1. Describe Freudian psychoanalysis and define its major features: free association, resistance, dream interpretation, and transference.
2. Explain how psychoanalysis is different today from how it was practiced by Freud.
3. Discuss the essential characteristics of client-centered therapy.
4. Describe the techniques used in behavior therapy, including systematic desensitization, flooding, aversion therapy, contingency management, contracting, and modeling.
5. Describe rational-emotive therapy and cognitive restructuring therapy.
6. Discuss the advantages of group therapy.
7. List two assumptions underlying family therapy.
8. Discuss the effectiveness of psychotherapy in general and whether any one type is more effective than others.
9. Discuss the problems resulting from deinstitutionalization.

VOCABULARY CHAPTER 13

On your own paper, write the definition for each of the following key terms. Your learning will be facilitated by writing the definition in your own words rather than copying the exact definition from your text.

PSYCHOSURGERY	LOBOTOMY
ELECTROCONVULSIVE THERAPY	ANTIPSYCHOTIC DRUGS
ANTIDEPRESSANT DRUGS	ANTIANXIETY DRUGS
PSYCHOANALYSIS	COGNITIVE RESTRUCTURING THERAPY
FREE ASSOCIATION	RESISTANCE
TRANSFERENCE	CLIENT-CENTERED THERAPY
EMPATHIC	BEHAVIOR THERAPY
SYSTEMATIC DESENSITIZATION	FLOODING
FAMILY THERAPY	AVERSION THERAPY
CONTINGENCY MANAGEMENT	CONTINGENCY CONTRACTING
MODELING	RATIONAL-EMOTIVE THERAPY

MATCHING TOPIC 13A, B

Match the following key terms from your textbook with the appropriate definitions.

____ 1. lobotomy		____ 2 resistance	
____ 3. electroconvulsive therapy		____ 4. psychosurgery	
____ 5. antianxiety drugs		____ 6. antidepressant drugs	
____ 7. antipsychotic drugs		____ 8. empathic	
____ 9. rational-emotive therapy		____ 10. family therapy	
____ 11. flooding		____ 12. modeling	
____ 13. aversion therapy		____ 14. systematic desensitization	
____ 15. free association		____ 16. client-centered therapy	
____ 17. transference		____ 18. behavior therapy	
____ 19. psychoanalysis		____ 20. contingency contracting	
____ 21. cognitive restructuring therapy		____ 22. contingency management	

a. The form of psychotherapy associated with Freud, aimed at helping the patient gain insight into unconscious conflicts.

b. A psychosurgical technique in which the prefrontal lobes of the cerebral cortex are severed from lower brain centers.

c. The procedure in psychoanalysis in which the patient is to express whatever comes to mind without editing responses.

d. In psychoanalysis, the inability or unwillingness to freely discuss some aspect of one's life.

e. In psychoanalysis, the situation in which the patient comes to feel about the analyst in the same way he or she once felt about some other important person.

f. The humanistic psychotherapy associated with Rogers, aimed at helping the client grow and change from within.

g. Able to understand and share the essence of another's feelings; to view from another's perspective.

h. Techniques of psychotherapy founded on principles of learning established in the psychological laboratory.

i. The application of classical conditioning procedures to alleviate anxiety in which anxiety-producing stimuli are paired with a state of relaxation.

j. An in vivo technique of behavior therapy in which the client is placed in the situation that most arouses a phobic reaction, and is prohibited from escaping.

k. Chemicals that are effective in reducing the experience of anxiety.

l. A technique of behavior therapy in which an aversive stimulus, such as a shock, is paired with an undesired behavior.

m. Bringing about changes in one's behaviors by controlling rewards or punishments.

n. Establishing a token economy of secondary reinforcers to reward appropriate behaviors.

o. The acquisition of new responses through the imitation of another who responds appropriately.

p. A form of cognitive therapy associated with Ellis, aimed at changing the subject's irrational beliefs or maladaptive cognitions.

q. A form of cognitive therapy, associated with Beck, in which patients are led to overcome negative self-images and pessimistic views of the future.

r. A variety of group therapy focusing on the roles, interdependence, and communication skills of family members.

s. A surgical procedure designed to affect one's psychological or behavioral reactions.

t. A treatment, usually for the symptoms of depression, in which an electric current passed through a patient's head causes a seizure and loss of consciousness.

u. Chemicals, such as chlorpromazine, that are effective in reducing psychotic symptoms.

v. Chemicals that reduce or eliminate the symptoms of depression.

TRUE-FALSE TEST TOPIC 13A

_____ 1. In ancient times, treatment of the mentally ill was primarily left up to the priests.

_____ 2. Socrates was among the first to suggest that mental illness had physical causes.

_____ 3. Oppression and persecution of the mentally ill peaked during the middle ages.

_____ 4. The first mental institution was the hospital in Paris where Phillipe Pinel unchained the insane.

_____ 5. Benjamin Rush is considered the father of American psychiatry.

_____ 6. Dorothea Dix was a nurse who campaigned for reform in both prisons and mental institutions.

_____ 7. Clifford Beers wrote a book about his experience in a mental hospital, prompting the mental health movement in the U.S.

_____ 8. Psychologists can prescribe drug treatment for their patients who only need antidepressants.

_____ 9. Both counseling psychologists and clinical psychologists usually have Ph.Ds.

_____ 10. At the present time, lobotomies are illegal.

_____ 11. One of the problems with ECT is that the beneficial effects are very short-lived.

_____ 12. The use of drugs to treat mental illness has been hailed as one of the most significant scientific achievements of the last half of the twentieth century.

_____ 13. One problem with antipsychotic drugs is that they only mask the symptoms which will usually return if the patient stops taking the medication.

_____ 14. Clozapine is an antipsychotic drug that appears to be effective in reducing both the positive and negative symptoms of schizophrenia.

_____ 15. Antidepressant drugs are often abused because they cause an exaggerated sense of euphoria and well-being in people who are not depressed.

TRUE-FALSE TEST TOPIC 13B

_____ 1. In all, there are only a few different types of psychotherapies.

_____ 2. Freud based psychoanalysis on assumptions related to conflict and the role of the unconscious mind.

_____ 3. According to Freud, the manifest content of dreams is the hidden or symbolic content.

_____ 4. Today psychoanalysis tends to be far briefer than when Freud practiced the technique.

_____ 5. The humanistic therapies share a concern for self-examination, personal growth, and development.

_____ 6. Gestalt therapy is a form of humanistic therapy associated with Carl Rogers.

_____ 7. Gestalt therapy is more directive than client-centered therapy.

_____ 8. Aversion therapy is most effective when used in conjunction with another form of therapy.

_____ 9. The contingency contracting technique is most effective with older adults in an open environment.

_____ 10. Cognitive therapists believe that a change in how a person thinks can bring about a change in the way the person acts.

_____ 11. Aaron Beck would be likely to describe his clients as optimists.

_____ 12. Beck's theory was most similar to Albert Ellis' cognitive theory.

_____ 13. Depression is a problem which responds well to cognitive restructuring therapy.

_____ 14. Only a trained psychoanalyst should conduct group therapy sessions.

_____ 15. About the only benefit to group therapy is saving a little money.

_____ 16. The applications of family therapy are usually limited to working with cases of alcoholism.

_____ 17. According to family therapists, it is very difficult for a therapist to bring about change in a child whose parents will not take part in therapy.

_____ 18. In general, there is some indication that family therapy is a better approach for many problems than individual therapy.

_____ 19. Research suggests that any form of psychotherapy is better than no treatment at all.

_____ 20. The National Institute of Mental Health estimates that 30 to 35 percent of homeless individuals have some type of psychological disorder.

FILL-IN TEST TOPIC 13A, B

1. The ancient Greeks and Romans typically left treatment of the mentally ill to the _____.

2. The first insane asylum was established in _____ toward the middle of the sixteenth century.

3. _____ _____ was the father of American psychiatry.

4. A _____ _____ usually does an internship at a psychiatric hospital or mental health center and has extensive background in psychological testing.

5. A psychiatrist is the only psychotherapist who can use biomedical therapies.

6. A _____ is a clinical psychologist or a psychiatrist who has additional training in Freudian psychoanalysis.

7. Surgical procedures designed to affect psychological reactions are called _____.

8. The _____ is a surgical procedure which severs the connections between the prefrontal lobes and the lower brain centers.

9. Electroconvulsive therapy is the more formal term for what are commonly called _____ _____.

10. It is now recommended that no more than _____ ECT treatments be given.

11. Chemicals that have their effect on the person's affect or behavior are collectively referred to as _____ _____.

12. Most antipsychotic drugs are prescribed for patients suffering from _____.

13. _____ drugs produce such side effects as dizziness, elevated blood pressure, sexual impotence, and liver damage.

14. _____ is most useful in the treatment of bipolar disorder.

15. Freud referred to the symbolic representation of the contents of the unconscious in dreams as _____ content.

16. According to Freud, _____ occurs when the patient unconsciously begins to feel about the analyst the same way he or she feels about some other important person, usually a parent.

17. A therapist who lets his or her feelings and past experiences interfere with his or her neutral and objective interactions with a patient is experiencing _____.

18. Carl Rogers founded _____ therapy.

19. _____ therapy could be described as methods of psychotherapeutic change founded on principles of learning established in the psychological laboratory.

166

20. In _____ _____ therapy the therapist controls rewards and punishments in an attempt to modify the patient's behavior.

21. A behavioral technique based on a token economy is called _____ _____.

22. The client's thoughts, perceptions, attitudes, and beliefs about himself are key factors in _____ therapies.

23. Aaron Beck's _____ _____ therapy is similar to RET, but less direct and confrontational.

24. In a move known as _____, mental patients were released from institutions and plans were made to treat them in community centers.

25. When a number of people are involved in a therapeutic setting at one time, it is referred to as _____ therapy.

MULTIPLE CHOICE TEST TOPIC 13A, B

1. Which of the following was NOT instrumental in the reform of the treatment of the mentally ill?
   a. Dorothea Dix
   b. Phillipe Pinel
   c. Sigmund Freud
   d. Clifford Beers

2. The turning point in the history of the treatment of the mentally ill which marked the beginning of enlightenment and better treatment was
   a. Hippocrate's declaration that mental illness has physical causes.
   b. the burning of the last witches early in the 17th century.
   c. an exorcism performed by Johann Sprenger.
   d. the unchaining of inmates in a French asylum.

3. The first person to perform a lobotomy was
   a. Pinel.
   b. Dix.
   c. Moniz.
   d. Freeman.

4. Which of the following would not be treated today with psychosurgery?
   a. chronic pain
   b. epilepsy
   c. depression
   d. dissociative identity disorder

5. Which of the following therapists may also be a psychoanalyst?
   a. licensed professional counselor
   b. clinical social worker
   c. psychiatrist
   d. pastoral counselor

6. The patients best suited for ECT (that is, those who seem to benefit most from this form of treatment) are those suffering from
   a. depression.
   b. depression and other psychotic symptoms such as hallucinations.
   c. anxiety-based disorders.
   d. schizophrenia.

7. The frequency of the use of ECT has been reduced due to
   a. the development of drug therapies.
   b. legal restrictions.
   c. the negative reputation of side effects.
   d. its general ineffectiveness.

8. Most antipsychotic drugs are used to treat
   a. anxiety-based disorders.
   b. depression.
   c. schizophrenia.
   d. suicidal patients.

9. Which of the following is NOT a problem regarding the use of antipsychotic drugs?
   a. There are certain patients for whom the drugs have no effect.
   b. The antipsychotic drugs can produce unpleasant and dangerous side effects.
   c. The symptoms are likely to return if the drugs are discontinued.
   d. In many cases the drugs actually cause symptoms to worsen.

10. Lithium is to _____ as clozapine is to schizophrenia.
    a. bipolar mood disorder
    b. depression
    c. anxiety-based disorders
    d. unipolar mood disorder

11. The single most prescribed antidepressant is
    a. clozapine.
    b. lithium.
    c. Prozac.
    d. Valium.

12. One difference between antipsychotic drugs and antidepressants is that antidepressants
    a. have no side effects.
    b. are more likely to bring about long-term cures.
    c. have a shorter duration of effect.
    d. can be bought over the counter without a prescription.

13. One real problem associated with antianxiety drugs is that they
    a. just aren't very effective.
    b. have tremendous negative side effects.
    c. can only be used with the mildest disorders.
    d. are so effective that the patient isn't motivated to deal with the source of the anxiety.

14. Which psychologist characterized a good therapist as being well-adjusted, warm, empathic, and supportive?
    a. Freud
    b. Beck
    c. Rogers
    d. Beutler

15. Which of the following therapies is associated with unconditional positive regard and a nondirective approach by the therapist?
    a. psychoanalysis
    b. client-centered therapy
    c. rational-emotive therapy
    d. cognitive therapy

16. Which of the following is NOT associated with Freudian psychoanalysis?
    a. free association
    b. empathy
    c. manifest dream content
    d. transference

17. Which of the following therapies was made popular by Albert Ellis?
    a. psychoanalysis
    b. client-centered therapy
    c. rational-emotive therapy
    d. cognitive therapy

18. Billy's father wants to help him get over his fear of the water, so he takes him to the local pool and gets into the water with him and will not let him out. This is an example of
    a. systematic desensitization.
    b. flooding.
    c. aversion therapy.
    d. parent training.

19. Bob went to a smoking cessation clinic where they had him chain smoke until he became ill. This would be an example of
    a. systematic desensitization.
    b. flooding.
    c. aversion therapy.
    d. parent training.

20. Albert Bandura is associated with the behavioral therapy approach known as
    a. contingency management.
    b. flooding.
    c. implosive therapy.
    d. modeling.

21. Two related assumptions guide the course of much family therapy. One assumption views each family member as a part of a system, while the other assumption stresses
    a. an even distribution of power and control.
    b. mutual attempts at reinforcing appropriate behaviors.
    c. the extent to which one's happiness depends on the other members of the family group.
    d. a concern for improved, open, and honest communication among family members.

22. Which of the following is NOT a problem associated with research to determine the effectiveness of psychotherapy?
    a. There is little data on how people would have responded without treatment.
    b. There is little agreement on what is meant by recovery.
    c. There are too many therapies to be compared with simple experiments.
    d. It is difficult to measure recovery or other benefits of therapy.

23. One advantage of group therapy is saving
    a. money.
    b. time.
    c. energy
    d. research.

24. Which of the following is NOT a correct match?
    a. Freud--psychoanalysis
    b. Rogers--client-centered therapy
    c. Beck--rational-emotive therapy
    d. Bandura--modeling

25. Which of the following is NOT a factor supporting the idea of deinstitutionalization?
    a. Concern for the rights of the patient.
    b. Avoiding the use of psychosurgery.
    c. The management of symptoms using drug therapy.
    d. The establishment of community mental health centers.

ESSENTIAL STRATEGIES FOR SUCCESS #13

STRESSED ABOUT THE TEST

Some people suffer from test anxiety so severe that it produces psychosomatic symptoms. Others experience poor performance along with anxiety. Whatever form it takes, test anxiety is unpleasant, but something can be done about it.

Research indicates that an overwhelming majority of test anxiety is related to poor preparation. The other study tips in this guide should help you to overcome this source of anxiety. If you are sure that you are preparing as well as possible and still experience test anxiety, try the following suggestions.

1. Get control of your breathing by focusing on it and counting as you inhale. Then exhale to the same slow count. You should feel much more in control and more relaxed.

2. Close your eyes and visualize a quiet, relaxing place, maybe a beach or a mountain scene. Think about how quiet and soothing the place is and how wonderful it is to be there in your mind. Repeat this as often as needed.

3. Spend some time thinking about why the exam is making you so anxious. What is it that you fear? Failure? Success? Being the last one finished? Disappointing someone? Disappointing yourself?

4. Listen to your self-talk. Is it negative? Do you say things to yourself like, "I'll never pass this test," or "I've always done poorly on essay exams." If so, stop this negative self-talk and replace it with positive messages such as "I am well prepared and know my material." "It doesn't matter if I finish last." "I know I can get this even if it takes a second try."

5. Finally, seek help for the test anxiety. Talk with your instructor or visit the student counseling center. Our counseling center runs free seminars every semester on test anxiety. Perhaps there is similar help available on your campus.

CHAPTER 14 — SOCIAL PSYCHOLOGY

LEARNING OBJECTIVES

The following items represent the fundamental concepts that you should know when you have finished studying this chapter. Read them now as a chapter preview and return to them to test your knowledge after you have studied.

Topic A
1. Define social psychology.
2. Define attitude and list the three components of an attitude.
3. Explain how attitudes are formed.
4. Define cognitive dissonance and explain how it relates to attitude change.
5. Discuss the central and peripheral routes in persuasive communication.
6. List the two basic types of attribution and explain how attribution becomes distorted or biased.
7. Describe the just world hypothesis, self-serving bias, and actor-observer bias.
8. Discuss the four theoretical models of interpersonal attraction.
9. Know the four determinants of interpersonal attraction and their effects.

Topic B
1. Discuss the methodology and findings of Asch's studies of conformity.
2. Discuss Milgram's research on obedience.
3. Explain how the presence of others affects helping behavior and list three factors that account for these effects.
4. Describe how social influence affects quality of performance.
5. Describe how social influence affects group decision-making.

VOCABULARY CHAPTER 14

On your own paper, write the definition for each of the following key terms. Your learning will be facilitated by writing the definition in your own words rather than copying the exact definition from your text.

ATTITUDE	SOCIAL PSYCHOLOGY
COGNITIVE DISSONANCE	CONFORMITY
SELF-SERVING BIAS	INTERNAL ATTRIBUTION

EXTERNAL ATTRIBUTION   FUNDAMENTAL ATTRIBUTION ERROR
JUST WORLD HYPOTHESIS   GROUPTHINK
ACTOR-OBSERVER BIAS   MERE EXPOSURE PHENOMENON
MATCHING PHENOMENON   GROUP POLARIZATION
SOCIAL INTERFERENCE   AUDIENCE INHIBITION
PLURALISTIC IGNORANCE   DIFFUSION OF RESPONSIBILITY
SOCIAL LOAFING   SOCIAL FACILITATION

MATCHING TOPIC 14A, B

Match the following key terms from your textbook with the appropriate definitions.

____ 1. self-serving bias	____ 2. internal attribution
____ 3. matching phenomenon	____ 4. mere exposure phenomenon
____ 5. social loafing	____ 6. pluralistic ignorance
____ 7. social interference	____ 8. cognitive dissonance
____ 9. just world hypothesis	____ 10. attitude
____ 11. fundamental attribution error	____ 12. social psychology
____ 13. group polarization	____ 14. social facilitation
____ 15. external attribution	____ 16. actor-observer bias
____ 17. diffusion of responsibility	____ 18. conformity
____ 19. groupthink	____ 20. audience inhibition

a. The tendency to attribute our successes to our own effort and ability and our failures to external, situational factors.

b. Impaired performance due to the presence of others.

c. A relatively stable and general evaluative disposition directed toward some object, consisting of feelings, behaviors, and beliefs.

d. The scientific study of how others influence the thoughts, feelings, and behaviors of the individual.

e. Improved performance due to the presence of others.

f. The tendency for a person to work less hard when part of a group in which everyone's efforts are pooled.

g. A motivating discomfort or tension caused by a lack of balance or consonance among one's cognitions.

h. The tendency for members of a group to give more extreme judgments following a discussion than they gave initially.

i. An explanation of behavior in terms of something within the person; a dispositional attribution.

j. An explanation of behavior in terms of something outside the person; a situational attribution.
k. The tendency to overuse internal attributions when explaining behavior.
l. The belief that the world is just and that people get what they deserve.
m. A style of thinking of cohesive groups concerned with maintaining agreement to the extent that independent ideas are discouraged.
n. The overuse of internal attributions to explain the behaviors of others and external attributions to explain our own behaviors.
o. The tendency to increase our liking of people and things the more we see of them.
p. The tendency to select partners whose level of physical attractiveness matches our own.
q. Changing one's behavior, under perceived pressure, so that it is consistent with the behavior of others.
r. Reluctance to intervene and offer assistance in front of others.
s. A condition in which the inaction of others leads each individual in a group to interpret a situation as a nonemergency, thus leading to general inactivity.
t. The tendency to allow others to share in the obligation to intervene.

TRUE-FALSE TEST TOPIC 14A

_____ 1. During the past 25 years, cognition has come to play an important role in social psychology.

_____ 2. One problem with the study of attitudes is that they tend to be unstable.

_____ 3. The behavioral component of attitudes is the most inconsistent.

_____ 4. It is possible that some attitudes are formed through the process of classical conditioning.

_____ 5. Festinger's research on cognitive dissonance suggests that if behavior is changed first, that changes in beliefs will follow.

_____ 6. The actual content of a communication is referred to as the central route.

_____ 7. There is a negative correlation between the perceived expertise of the communicator and the actual persuasion that occurs.

_____ 8. If a person tends to disregard situational factors in favor of internal, dispositional factors, he or she might be making the fundamental attribution error.

_____ 9. The idea that victims got what they deserved is an example of actor-observer bias.

_____ 10. According to the reinforcement model of attraction, we tend to like people whom we associate with rewards or reinforcement.

_____ 11. According to attachment theory, one's style of relating to others is very stable throughout the lifespan.

_____ 12. According to the principle of reciprocity, we are most attracted to the people who like us now but did not like us originally.

_____ 13. The effects of the matching phenomenon appear to apply only to opposite sex relationships.

_____ 14. According to Byrne's research, the old adage that opposites attract is probably not true.

_____ 15. According to the mere exposure phenomenon, familiarity does breed contempt.

TRUE-FALSE TEST TOPIC 14B

_____ 1. Conformity is always undesirable and negative.

_____ 2. Asch found that conformity increased as the size of the incorrect majority increased.

_____ 3. Asch found that subjects were more likely to trust their own judgment if one other person among the confederates agreed with them.

_____ 4. The astonishing results of Milgram's study indicated that the subjects responded to the authority figures and were not at all distressed when required to administer what they thought were painful shocks.

_____ 5. When Milgram repeated his initial study using women as subjects, he found that women were much less likely to obey.

_____ 6. Following his study, Milgram provided reasonable care for his subjects, doing all that was necessary for them.

_____ 7. There are really no realistic or reasonable excuses for failure to help in an emergency.

_____ 8. According to Latane and Darley, the victim is unlikely to get help in an emergency because of all the steps in deciding to render assistance and the potential costs of intervention.

_____ 9. A review of the research on the bystander effect indicates that this is a very consistent phenomenon and not just the results of a few isolated events.

_____ 10. Social loafing tends to decline when individuals believe that their effort is special or that it can be identified and evaluated.

_____ 11. Group polarization refers to the fact that group discussion usually leads to a more conservative conclusion than the opinions of the individuals in the group.

_____ 12. Demographic statistics for the next decade suggest that violent crimes are likely to continue to increase.

FILL-IN TEST TOPIC 14A

1. _____ _____ involves the study of how other people affect the psychological reactions of the individual.

2. A relatively stable and general evaluative disposition toward some object consisting of beliefs, feelings, and behaviors defines a/an _____.

3. Attitudes may be formed through classical conditioning, operant conditioning, or _____ _____.

4. _____ _____ occurs when there is inconsistency between a person's thoughts or beliefs and behavior.

5. _____ conducted research on cognitive dissonance suggesting that behavior can be changed by changing attitudes first.

6. The _____ route in persuasive communication refers to the way the message is presented.

7. In attribution theory, _____ attributions explain the source of behavior in terms of some characteristic of the person.

8. _____ attributions explain the sources of behavior in terms of the situation or social context.

9. The _____ _____ error is the tendency to disregard dispositional factors when we make judgments about behavior.

10. According to the _____ model of interpersonal attraction, we are attracted to people that we associate with rewards.

11. _____ theory suggests that interpersonal relationships can be classified into one of three types depending on the attitudes one has about such relationships.

12. Liking and valuing people who like and value us is referred to as _____.

13. The _____ phenomenon reflects the likelihood that individuals will usually select partners whose level of attractiveness are similar to their own.

FILL-IN TEST TOPIC 14B

1. Modifying behavior under pressure in order to be consistent with the behavior of others is known as _____.

2. Yielding to the perceived pressure of peers is conformity, but yielding to the perceived pressure of an authority figure is _____.

3. The Yale psychologist who became interested in and did research on obedience was _____.

4. After a study such as Milgram's, it is very important that subjects be _____, explaining to them the deceptions involved and why they were necessary.

5. First attempts at explaining why no one intervened to help Kitty Genovese used labels such as _____ and alienation.

6. The first step in bystander intervention is for the bystander to _____ the situation.

7. The tendency to be hesitant in doing things in front of others is referred to as _____ _____.

8. _____ ____ _____ refers to the fact that a single bystander will respond more quickly to an emergency, but a witness who is part of a group shares that responsibility with the others.

9. _____ and Darley have contributed significantly to research concerning bystander intervention and other related phenomena such as diffusion of responsibility and pluralistic ignorance.

10. The tendency to work less as the size of the work group increases is called _____ _____.

11. The opposite of social interference is _____ _____.

12. According to _____, both social facilitation and social interference are related to increased arousal caused by the presence of others.

13. _____ _____ refers to the process of making an individual's decisions more extreme as a function of group decision making.

MULTIPLE CHOICE TEST TOPIC 14A

1. Social psychology can be defined as the study of
   a. how people influence the thoughts, feelings, and behaviors of an individual.
   b. how people interact in groups.
   c. a person's behavior in social situations.
   d. why people form institutions and join groups or associations.

2. During the past 25 years, the field of psychology has taken on a _____ influence.
   a. behaviorist
   b. existential
   c. cognitive
   d. humanistic

3. If you buy only products that are made in the United States, you are demonstrating the _____ component of attitudes.
   a. affective
   b. cognitive
   c. intentional
   d. behavioral

4. The _____ component of attitudes is the most controversial because people don't always act on their beliefs.
   a. affective
   b. cognitive
   c. intentional
   d. behavioral

5. Advertising that relies on testimonials from satisfied customers is relying on forming attitudes through
   a. operant conditioning.
   b. classical conditioning.
   c. observational learning.
   d. persuasion.

6. Randy left his car door unlocked and his car was subsequently stolen. Some of his coworkers said, "he got what he deserved." The coworkers' attitudes exemplify the
   a. self-serving bias.
   b. actor-observer bias.
   c. fundamental attribution error.
   d. just world hypothesis.

7. The social psychologist who conducted research regarding cognitive dissonance was
   a. Festinger.
   b. Zajonc.
   c. Darley.
   d. Miller.

8. The research on cognitive dissonance suggests that one way to change people's attitudes is to
   a. have them read testimonials from others who have made similar changes.
   b. provide models who have successfully made similar changes.
   c. get them to change their behaviors first.
   d. subject them to brainwashing.

9. A student who attributes his good grades to his own brilliance and hard work, and his bad grades to poor teachers illustrates the
   a. self-serving bias.
   b. actor-observer bias.
   c. fundamental attribution error.
   d. just world hypothesis.

10. According to the _____ model of interpersonal attraction, a relationship is in danger if one person feels that he or she is getting more from a relationship than is deserved.
    a. attachment
    b. equity
    c. social exchange
    d. reinforcement

11. Ben was interested in agriculture and wanted to become a rancher. While in high school, he dated a girl that he nicknamed "five hundred acres" because her father owned a lot of land. One explanation for his attraction to her would be the _____ model.
    a. social exchange
    b. reinforcement
    c. equity
    d. attachment

12. According to attachment theory, one's style of forming attachments is
    a. established after several different stages.
    b. relatively stable throughout the lifespan.
    c. changeable and subject to the influence of life events.
    d. totally unpredictable.

13. The matching phenomenon suggests that when rejection is a real possibility, people choose partners who are similar to themselves in
    a. ethnicity.
    b. socioeconomic status.
    c. physical attractiveness.
    d. age.

14. Which of the following is NOT one of the four determinants of interpersonal attraction?
    a. proximity
    b. similarity
    c. reciprocity
    d. generosity

15. The _____ principle of interpersonal attraction suggests that we tend to like those people who like us.
    a. proximity
    b. similarity
    c. reciprocity
    d. generosity

MULTIPLE CHOICE TEST TOPIC 14B

1. In the study of social influence, psychologists are most interested in how
   a. an individual influences another individual.
   b. an individual influences a group of people.
   c. groups of people influence individuals.
   d. groups of people influence other groups of people.

2. A confederate in a research study is someone who is
   a. "in on the experiment" and assists the researcher.
   b. in the control group.
   c. in the experimental group.
   d. observing the study in order to maintain ethical standards.

3. Asch is to conformity as Milgram is to _____.
   a. obedience
   b. perception
   c. social influence
   d. authority

4. It is very unlikely that Milgram's studies will ever be repeated because
   a. it is unnecessary when research results are so conclusive.
   b. some of the subjects in the learner role were permanently impaired.
   c. ethical standards have been raised and would prohibit such a study today.
   d. no one would voluntarily participate in such a study.

5. According to research on bystander intervention, which of the following people is most likely to render aid in an emergency?
   a. a single bystander
   b. a single bystander with experience in similar emergencies
   c. a member of a large crowd of bystanders
   d. the first person who happens by

6. The tendency to be hesitant to do things in front of others is referred to as
   a. pluralistic ignorance.
   b. social interference.
   c. bystander intervention.
   d. audience inhibition.

7. Scott participates in speed skating events. His father has been keeping records of his performances and notes that he skates faster when competing against other skaters as opposed to skating against the clock. The best explanation for this is
    a. bystander effect.
    b. social facilitation.
    c. social interference.
    d. social loafing.

8. Which of the following is NOT an example of an effect that would lead a person to fail to help in an emergency?
    a. diffusion of responsibility
    b. social loafing
    c. audience inhibition
    d. pluralistic ignorance

9. According to Zajonc, social facilitation occurs when the behavior in question is
    a. simple, routine, or well-learned.
    b. complex and well-practiced.
    c. novel and easy to learn.
    d. adequately rehearsed.

10. A jury enters the jury room to deliberate with all of its members having moderate confidence in the defendant's guilt. After deliberations, and having found the defendant guilty, indeed, the jurors are even more convinced of the defendant's guilt. This illustrates the phenomenon known as
    a. group polarization.
    b. groupthink.
    c. social facilitation.
    d. opinion drift.

ESSENTIAL STRATEGIES FOR SUCCESS #14

SOCIAL COGNITION: STUDYING WITH OTHER PEOPLE

There appears to be three options for studying in terms of a social context: studying with better students, studying with students at about your same level, and tutoring or helping weaker students. Let's examine these options in a little more detail.

Your first step should be an honest evaluation of yourself as a student or "studier." Do you have good skills? Are you self-motivated? Are you well-organized? Are you able to stay on task or are you easily distracted? Do you make good grades? What do you have to offer a study partner? Once you have answered some of these questions, you are ready to think about whether you would benefit from a study group or study partner and what kind of person/people you should seek.

If you are a weak student, you should seek out a stronger student who will help you to select the main points, get organized, motivated, and stay on task. There is little to be gained by assembling a group of weak students.

A strong student can really benefit by tutoring or helping others. Research indicates that peer tutors benefit more from the experience than the person who receives the tutoring. The best explanation for this is that the process of organizing the information and understanding it well enough to explain it to someone else, enhancing the tutor's own understanding and memory.

If you are an average student, you should seek out other average students or stronger students as study partners. Whatever your level, the following guidelines should be helpful.

1.   Try to meet several people on the first day of class and get their phone numbers. You will want to call them about notes and assignments if you should be unable to attend class.

2.   Look around to see who is taking notes. Try to find someone who appears to be organized. Listen for someone who asks intelligent, thought-provoking questions or offers relevant, interesting comments in class. Another hint: good students tend to sit near the front of class.

3.   Once you have formed a study group, always have a definite plan as to what you want to accomplish when the group meets. If necessary, set an agenda just like a business meeting and stick to it. Do NOT let the study session turn into a "bull" session.

4. Go to the group well-prepared. Read assignments and write out questions ahead of time. Make notes about issues you want to clarify or discuss with the group. This should not be a substitute for individual effort, rather a way to enhance your own preparation.
5. Reward yourselves if you are successful. Raise your test grades? Then go out and celebrate.

CHAPTER 15—INDUSTRIAL/ORGANIZATIONAL, ENVIRONMENTAL, AND SPORTS PSYCHOLOGY

LEARNING OBJECTIVES

The following items represent the fundamental concepts that you should know when you have finished studying this chapter. Read them now as a chapter preview and return to them to test your knowledge after you have studied.

Topic A
1. Explain what is involved in doing a job analysis.
2. Describe some of the information sources that can be used in making personnel decisions.
3. List some of the factors that need to be considered in the design, implementation, and evaluation of a training program.
4. Summarize some of the factors that affect motivation of workers to do a good job.
5. Discuss the various factors related to job satisfaction.
6. Describe the relationship between job satisfaction and job productivity.
7. Discuss safety in the workplace.

Topic B
1. Define environmental psychology and list some of the issues that environmental psychologists study.
2. Define the concepts of personal space and territoriality.
3. Explain the difference between population density and crowding.
4. List the positive and negative aspects of city living.
5. Describe the effects of noise, extreme temperature, and neurotoxins on behavior.
6. Discuss some of the ways that psychologists can become involved in sports and athletics.

VOCABULARY CHAPTER 15

On your own paper, write the definition for each of the following key terms. Your learning will be facilitated by writing the definition in your own words rather than copying the exact definition from your text.

JOB ANALYSIS	PERFORMANCE CRITERIA
EXPECTANCY THEORY	EQUITY THEORY
JOB SATISFACTION	ENVIRONMENTAL PSYCHOLOGY
PERSONAL SPACE	TERRITORIALITY
POPULATION DENSITY	CROWDING
NEUROTOXINS	NOISE
SPORT PSYCHOLOGY	

MATCHING TOPIC 15A, B

Match the following key terms from your textbook with the appropriate definitions.

_____ 1. neurotoxins   _____ 2. population density
_____ 3. expectancy theory   _____ 4. performance criteria
_____ 5. equity theory   _____ 6. personal space
_____ 7. job satisfaction   _____ 8. job analysis
_____ 9. crowding   _____ 10. sports psychology
_____ 11. noise   _____ 12. environmental psychology
_____ 13. territoriality

a. A complete and specific description of a job, including the qualities required to do it well.

b. Specific behaviors or characteristics that a person should have in order to do a job as well as possible.

c. Intrusive, unwanted, or excessive experience of sound.

d. Chemicals that affect psychological processes through the nervous system.

e. The subjective feeling of discomfort caused by a sense of lack of space.

f. The view that workers make logical choices to do what they believe will result in their attaining outcomes of highest value.

g. The view that workers are motivated to match their inputs and outcomes with those fellow workers in similar positions.

h. An attitude; a collection of feelings about one's job or job experiences.

i. A quantitative measure of the number of persons per unit of area.

j. The application of psychological principles to sport and physical activity at all levels of skill development.

k. The field of applied psychology that studies the effect of the general environment on organisms within it.

l. The mobile "bubble" of space around you reserved for intimate relationships into which others may enter only by invitation.

m. The setting off and marking of a piece of territory as one's own.

TRUE-FALSE TEST TOPIC 15A

_____ 1. A job analysis describes the actual behaviors done on the job in more detail than a job description.

_____ 2. Most job analyses involve the use of both hard and soft criteria.

_____ 3. The goal of a job analysis is to find the best available person to do a job as well as possible.

_____ 4. Job application forms are really outdated and provide little useful information.

_____ 5. It is possible to train people to be better interviewers.

_____ 6. Unstructured interviews tend to be more valid than structured interviews.

_____ 7. The most useful psychological tests are those that assess some sort of cognitive function.

_____ 8. Situational testing involves role playing some function of the job in question.

_____ 9. Although training is a frequently used approach to improving productivity, in reality its effectiveness is limited.

_____ 10. One crucial aspect of a training program is some means of evaluating its effectiveness.

_____ 11. Motivation is of concern to the I/O psychologist because being able to do a job well and wanting to do a job well are not the same thing.

_____ 12. According to equity theory, the reality of fairness is more important than the perception of fairness.

_____ 13. The younger the worker, the more likely that person is to be satisfied with a job.

_____ 14. There tend to be large racial differences in job satisfaction.

_____ 15. In general, the lower the status of the job, the lower the job satisfaction.

TRUE-FALSE TEST TOPIC 15B

_____ 1. Environmental psychologists have concluded that living in a densely populated city produces negative consequences such as increased stress.

_____ 2. Personal space and territory are the same thing.

_____ 3. Territoriality was first studied in nonhumans.

_____ 4. In general, public distance involves the longest actual distance for personal space.

_____ 5. City living does appear to have some advantages over living in the country.

_____ 6. Noise is considered most stressful when it is loud, high-pitched, and unpredictable.

_____ 7. Although the presence of noise has been proven to disrupt performance on problem-solving tasks, the performance returns to normal as soon as the noise stimulus is removed.

_____ 8. It seems clear that extreme temperatures have adverse effects on behavior.

_____ 9. Although some environmental toxins affect physical health, there are none known that affect mental health or behavior.

_____ 10. Analyzing the psychological characteristics of athletes and maximizing the performance of athletes are two applications of psychology to sports.

FILL-IN TEST TOPIC 15A

1. A _____ _____ is a systematic study of the tasks, duties, and responsibilities of a job and the knowledge, skills, and abilities needed to perform it.

2. Performance criteria that are subjective in nature are referred to as _____ criteria.

3. A person who does employment interviews should be aware of the influence of _____.

4. When applicants are asked to role play the task they may be hired to do, it is referred to as _____ _____.

5. When choosing a test for use in personnel selection, _____ of the test is a very important consideration.

190

6. _____ theory suggests that workers make work-related decisions according to their beliefs and expectations.

7. Equity theory is associated with _____.

8. The greatest research emphasis in the area of worker motivation is placed on _____.

9. _____ _____ refers to a person's attitude toward work, usually a pleasurable or positive feeling.

10. Marital status, _____, and size of work group are better predictors of absenteeism than job satisfaction.

FILL-IN TEST TOPIC 15B

1. _____ psychology is the subfield that studies how the general environment affects the behavior and mental processes of those living in it.

2. The imaginary bubble of space that surrounds a person and into which others may enter comfortably only by invitation, is called _____ _____.

3. The smallest amount or bubble of personal space is between actual contact and about 18 inches and is referred to as _____ distance.

4. A distance of 4 to 12 feet is referred to as _____ distance.

5. _____ involves the setting off and marking of a piece of territory as one's own.

6. A teenager's bedroom is a prime example of _____ territory.

7. The number of persons or animals per unit of area is referred to as _____ _____.

8. Substances that have harmful effects on the human nervous system are called _____.

9. _____ psychology is the application of psychology to sport and physical activity at all levels of skill development.

10. The sport of _____ appears to be one in which the performer may experience the phenomenon of getting a "hot hand."

MULTIPLE CHOICE TEST TOPIC 15A

1. All psychologists are interested in the ABCs: affect, behavior, and cognitions. Which of the following distinguishes the work of an industrial psychologist from psychologists in other fields?
   a. An interest in the ABCs as applied to work settings.
   b. Using the ABCs to train good employees.
   c. Applying the ABCs to institutions.
   d. A focus more on behavior and less on affect and cognition.

2. The two steps in writing a job analysis are
   a. interviewing people in the job and reporting their ideas about the job.
   b. making a complete description of what the person is expected to do and translating the duties into measurable criteria.
   c. measuring what the person actually does and determining what changes should be made.
   d. making a survey of the supervisors and compiling the survey results.

3. Which of the following would not be a part of selecting the best person for the job?
   a. job application
   b. interview
   c. psychological testing
   d. psychoanalysis

4. When psychological tests are used in personnel selection, an important concern regarding the tests is
   a. cost.
   b. ease of administration.
   c. validity.
   d. objectivity.

5. When I/O psychologists use psychological tests, it is usually to
   a. screen out job applicants who have psychological disorders.
   b. find psychological traits known to be correlated with job success.
   c. ensure that only the most intelligent applicants will be considered for the job.
   d. help determine which criteria of the job analysis are going to be most useful.

6. Which of the following would not be an important aspect of evaluating a training program?
   a. evaluate at different levels
   b. include both short-term and long-term evaluation
   c. expend great effort at the beginning assessing organizational needs and establishing training objectives
   d. develop the philosophy that some training is better than no training

7. Which of the following would typically be used to evaluate a training program?
   a. ask participants how they feel about the training
   b. measure the behavioral changes that follow the training
   c. measure increases in profit or productivity
   d. all of the above

8. Expectancy theory is typically associated with
   a. Vroom.
   b. Watson.
   c. Adams.
   d. Locke.

9. In order for goal setting to have a positive influence on a worker's behavior, which of the following criteria must be met?
   a. The employee must set the goal himself or herself.
   b. The goal must be clear to the employee.
   c. The employee must think of the goal as worth the effort.
   d. Both b and c.

10. Which of the following is NOT true of goal setting as a means of motivating employees?
   a. Difficult but achievable goals increase productivity more than easy goals.
   b. Specific goals are better than general ones.
   c. Periodical feedback is not necessary with highly motivated workers.
   d. It doesn't especially matter who sets the goal, as long as the employee thinks it is reasonable and worthwhile.

11. Which of the following statements regarding job satisfaction is NOT true?
   a. Younger workers tend to be more satisfied with their jobs than older workers.
   b. Men and women aren't very different in regard to job satisfaction.
   c. Racial differences in job satisfaction are small.
   d. Job satisfaction is related to the perceived status of one's job.

12. Which of the following work behaviors is most related to job satisfaction?
   a. productivity
   b. efficiency
   c. absenteeism
   d. motivation

MULTIPLE CHOICE TEST TOPIC 15B

1. Which of the following is the least influential factor related to personal space?
   a. who the intruder is
   b. your age
   c. your sex
   d. your cultural background

2. You are being audited by the IRS and have never met the auditor. Which of the descriptors below indicates the amount of personal space with which you are most likely to be comfortable. (Note that being in Brazil is not an option.)
   a. intimate distance
   b. personal distance
   c. social distance
   d. pubic distance

3. My family has rented a pavilion in a local park to use for a family reunion. This is an example of _____ territory.
   a. primary.
   b. secondary.
   c. public.
   d. private.

4. Which of the following are functions of various territories that we devise?
   a. They provide a sense of structure and continuity.
   b. They help us claim some sense of identity.
   c. They regulate and reinforce our need for privacy.
   d. All of the above.

5. When comparing the costs and the benefits of city life, it appears that
   a. city life is definitely inferior to country living.
   b. city life is worse for those who don't have other options.
   c. city life really has no advantages over country life.
   d. city life would be fine if the noise and air pollution problems were solved.

6. Two important factors in whether noise disrupts performance are
   a. predictability and control.
   b. pitch and predictability.
   c. control and frequency of the noise.
   d. ear protection and frequency of exposure.

7. The common perception that high temperatures are associated with more aggressive behavior and displays of violence is
   a. a myth promoted by policemen to get more recruits during summer months.
   b. an opinion not supported by research.
   c. largely supported by research.
   d. none of the above.

8. According to research, an athlete might be expected to score higher on
   a. anxiety.
   b. depression.
   c. aggression.
   d. fatigue.

9. Which of the following best summarizes the research on characteristics of athletes?
   a. When general trends are sought, they are generally not found.
   b. More differences appear in male athletes than in female athletes.
   c. Differences are more apparent in sports that are significantly different, such as hockey and billiards.
   d. Athletes are substantially different from nonathletes in significant ways.

10. Mental rehearsal is useful in all of the following EXCEPT
    a. the rehearsal of a particular behavior pattern.
    b. reducing anxiety concerning performance.
    c. reducing negative thoughts about the performance.
    d. setting realistic goals.

ESSENTIAL STRATEGIES FOR SUCCESS #15

ADD SOME COLOR TO YOUR STUDYING

You may already be aware that the single most effective study strategy is highlighting or underlining in textbooks. Here are some hints for making this technique even more effective.

1. Don't underline mindlessly. Read carefully before you highlight or underline anything. Then limit your marking to those things you do not know. There is no sense marking a key term if it is one with which you are already familiar.

2. Use color coding to identify different kinds of information. When you go back for a study session, you may find that you wish to review only key terms on one occasion and important people in psychology on another. To prepare for this, use one color to highlight key terms and another for important figures.

3. Another area that might be identified with a different color is important research studies and their results.

4. Can you think of additional ways to segment information for studying? If so, incorporate them into your new color coding system.

5. When you study each segment that you have color coded, you should begin to identify information that you know and other segments that still need more study. Develop a system for separating these by marking what you know with an asterisk or a check mark. When you study again, focus on the material which is not marked. In this manner, you are constantly making your learning task smaller and revealing to yourself the proven results of your previous study sessions.

STATISTICAL APPENDIX

LEARNING OBJECTIVES

The following items represent the fundamental concepts that you should know when you have finished studying this chapter. Read them now as a chapter preview and return to them to test your knowledge after you have studied.

1. Define a frequency distribution and a histogram, and explain what each is used for.
2. List and define three measures of central tendency.
3. Define standard deviation.
4. Explain what is meant by "test of statistical significance."
5. Explain the normal curve and the percentage of cases at each standard deviation.

STATISTICS VOCABULARY

On your own paper, write the definition for each of the following key terms. Your learning will be facilitated by writing the definition in your own words rather than copying the exact definition from your text.

FREQUENCY DISTRIBUTION   HISTOGRAM
CENTRAL TENDENCY   VARIABILITY
MEAN   MEDIAN
MODE   RANGE
STANDARD DEVIATION   INFERENTIAL STATISTICS
NORMAL CURVE   STATISTICALLY SIGNIFICANT
DIFFERENCES
VARIANCE

MATCHING

Match the following key terms from your textbook with the appropriate definitions.

_____ 1. normal curve   _____ 2. inferential statistics
_____ 3. range   _____ 4. standard deviation
_____ 5. histogram   _____ 6. variability
_____ 7. frequency distribution   _____ 8. central tendency
_____ 9. mode   _____ 10. mean
_____ 11. median   _____ 12. statistically significant difference

a. An ordered listing of all X values, indicating the frequency with which each occurs.

b. A bar graph, a graphic representation of a frequency distribution.

c. A measure of the middle, or average, score in a set.

d. The extent of spread or dispersion in a set or distribution of scores.

e. The sum of all X scores divided by the number of X scores.

f. The score of an ordered set above which and below which fall half the scores.

g. The most frequently occurring X value in a set.

h. The highest score in a distribution minus the lowest score.

i. A type of average of the deviations of each X score from the mean of the distribution.

j. Statistical tests that tell us about the significance of the results of experimental or correlational studies.

k. Differences between descriptive statistics not likely to have occurred by chance if the descriptive statistics were describing the same group.

l. A commonly found, symmetrical, bell-shaped frequency distribution.

TRUE-FALSE TEST

_____ 1. Graphs of frequencies of scores are among the most common types of graphs used in psychology.

_____ 2. The mean, median, and mode are all measures of variability.

_____ 3. The normal curve is a rare, asymmetrical frequency distribution.

_____ 4. The range and the standard deviation are measures of variability.

_____ 5. The normal curve could be thought of as a line graph for a frequency distribution.

_____ 6. Scores in a distribution that form a normal curve tend to bunch around the standard deviation.

_____ 7. In a normal curve, all the measures of central tendency, the mean, median, and the mode would be the same numerical value.

_____ 8. The mean divides the normal curve exactly in half.

_____ 9. Mean IQ is 115.

_____ 10. All normal curves have the same amount of variability.

FILL-IN TEST

1. A _____ _____ lists all the numbers or scores and indicates the frequency with which each occurs.

2. A graphical representation of a frequency distribution is called a/an _____.

3. The _____ is the middle score in a distribution.

4. The _____ is the central tendency measure that is most often used in statistics.

5. The most frequently occurring value in a data set is the _____.

6. The _____ _____ is a measure of variability that tells us the average amount by which scores deviate from their mean.

7. _____ statistics are tests that tell us about the significance of the results of experiments.

8. A commonly found, symmetrical bell-shaped frequency distribution is called the _____ _____.

9. Differences between descriptive statistics not likely to have occurred by chance are said to be _____ _____.

10. A measure of variability based on the highest and lowest values in the distribution is the _____.

MULTIPLE CHOICE TEST

1. Statistics can best be described as
   a. tools.
   b. lies.
   c. another form of mathematics.
   d. much ado about nothing.

2. Which of the following is NOT a measure of central tendency?
   a. mean.
   b. median.
   c. mode.
   d. standard deviation.

3. Averages are referred to as measures of
   a. variability.
   b. correlation.
   c. reliability.
   d. central tendency.

4. To determine how much dispersion is in a particular set of scores, researchers focus on
   a. variability.
   b. correlation.
   c. reliability.
   d. central tendency.

5. The range is a measure of variability that has the weakness of
   a. being a large number.
   b. only considering two values in the set.
   c. causing the overestimation of variability.
   d. causing the underestimation of variability.

6. Formulas that allow the researcher to calculate the likelihood that particular experimental or correlational results arose by chance are referred to as
   a. descriptive statistics.
   b. inferential statistics.
   c. advanced statistics.
   d. measures of central tendency.

7. Results that seem unlikely to have occurred by chance are said to be
    a. positively correlated.
    b. nonstatistical.
    c. negatively correlated.
    d. statistically significant.

8. Which of the following is/are factors that influence a test of significance?
    a. size of the mean difference
    b. sample size
    c. variability
    d. all of the above

9. In a normal curve, the symmetry allows us to know that _____ percent of the values in the distribution fall between one standard deviation below the mean and one standard deviation above the mean.
    a. 34
    b. 50
    c. 68
    d. 84

10. If mean IQ is 100 and the standard deviation is 15, what percent of people will have IQs between 85 and 100?
    a. 10
    b. 28
    c. 34
    d. 50

ESSENTIAL STRATEGIES FOR SUCCESS #16

USE IT OR LOSE IT

Below you will find a list of the fifteen study strategies that have been presented in the previous chapters. Perhaps they will not all be equally helpful to you. It is certain, that none will be helpful unless tried and evaluated. After you have given each strategy a fair trial, write a one sentence evaluation in the space provided. Try to identify several strategies that have helped you the most and make them part of your regular study routine.

1. Time management.

2. Dealing with distractions.

3. Getting to know your textbook.

4. How to read a textbook.

5. Using the Premack Principle to reinforce studying.

6. Getting along with your professor.

7. Using mnemonic strategies.

8. Using 3 x 5 cards.

9. Being a star in class.

10. Suggestions for taking notes.

11. Taking objective tests.

12. Taking essay exams.

13. Stressed about the test.

14. Studying with other people.

15. Adding some color to your studying.

ANSWER SECTION

CHAPTER 1

CHAPTER 1 MATCHING

1. M	2. J	3. G	4. D	5. Z
6. BB	7. Q	8. P	9. I	10. X
11. L	12. V	13. S	14. N	15. GG
16. T	17. U	18. R	19. W	20. Y
21. F	22. H	23. E	24. C	25. K
26. A	27. DD	28. B	29. O	30. AA
31. CC	32. FF	33. EE		

CHAPTER 1 TRUE-FALSE TEST TOPIC 1A

1. F	2. F	3. T	4. F	5. T
6. T	7. T	8. T	9. T	10. F
11. T	12. F	13. T	14. T	15. T

CHAPTER 1 TRUE-FALSE TEST TOPIC 1B

1. T	2. T	3. T	4. F	5. F
6. T	7. T	8. T	9. T	10. F

CHAPTER 1 FILL-IN TEST TOPIC 1A

1. science
2. hypothesis
3. behavior
4. interactive dualism
5. Locke
6. von Helmholtz
7. Wundt
8. functionalism
9. Margaret Floy Washburn
10. Mary Calkins
11. John Watson
12. Freud
13. whole
14. humanistic
15. Personality

CHAPTER 1 FILL-IN TEST TOPIC 1B

1. naturalistic observation
2. sample
3. case history
4. negative
5. experimental
6. random assignment
7. confidentiality
8. American Psychological Association
9. nature, nurture
10. Phenomenology

CHAPTER 1 MULTIPLE CHOICE TEST TOPIC 1A

1. B	2. A	3. D	4. B	5. C
6. C	7. B	8. C	9. B	10. A
11. D	12. D	13. B		

CHAPTER 1 MULTIPLE CHOICE TEST TOPIC 1B

1. B	2. D	3. A	4. A	5. C
6. D	7. A	8. A	9. B	10. C
11. C	12. D			

CHAPTER 2

CHAPTER 2 MATCHING TOPIC 2A

1. F	2. O	3. B	4. M	5. G
6. C	7. J	8. I	9. D	10. L
11. N	12. A	13. H	14. E	15. K
16. K				

CHAPTER 2 MATCHING TOPIC 2B

1. G	2. K	3. L	4. O	5. J
6. F	7. C	8. T	9. V	10. X
11. Q	12. P	13. B	14. Z	15. A
16. R	17. D	18. U	19. AA	20. BB
21. W	22. E	23. M	24. S	25. Y
26. H	27. N	28. I		

CHAPTER 2 TRUE-FALSE TEST TOPIC 2A

1. F	2. T	3. T	4. F	5. T
6. T	7. T	8. T	9. F	10. F
11. T				

CHAPTER 2 TRUE-FALSE TEST TOPIC 2B

1. F	2. F	3. T	4. F	5. T
6. F	7. F	8. T	9. F	10. F
11. T	12. T			

CHAPTER 2 FILL-IN TEST TOPIC 2A
1. axon terminals
2. myelin
3. neuron
4. Chemical ions
5. resting potential
6. synapse
7. vesicles
8. neural threshold
9. dopamine
10. Endorphins

CHAPTER 2 FILL-IN TEST TOPIC 2B
1. central nervous system
2. hormones
3. parasympathetic
4. spinal reflexes
5. peripheral
6. sympathetic
7. dorsal
8. spinal reflex
9. brain stem
10. cross-laterality
11. reticular activating system
12. hippocampus
13. association
14. epilepsy

CHAPTER 2 MULTIPLE CHOICE TEST TOPIC 2A
1. B 2. H 3. A 4. A 5. D
6. A 7. D 8. C 9. D 10. C
11. B 12. B

CHAPTER 2 MULTIPLE CHOICE TEST TOPIC 2B
1. B 2. A 3. B 4. B 5. C
6. C 7. A 8. D 9. D 10. A
11. B 12. A 13. C

CHAPTER 3

CHAPTER 3 MATCHING
1. C 2. H 3. A 4. G 5. D
6. P 7. S 8. U 9. I 10. B
11. F 12. K 13. O 14. W 15. M
16. R 17. J 18. N 19. L 20. Q
21. V 22. E 23. T

CHAPTER 3 TRUE-FALSE TEST TOPIC 3A
1. T	2. F	3. T	4. T	5. F
6. F	7. F	8. F	9. T	10. T

CHAPTER 3 TRUE-FALSE TEST TOPIC 3B
1. F	2. T	3. T	4. T	5. T
6. F	7. F	8. F	9. F	10. T
11. F	12. T			

CHAPTER 3 TRUE-FALSE TEST TOPIC 3C
1. T	2. T	3. F	4. T	5. T
6. F	7. F	8. F	9. F	10. F
11. F	12. T	13. T	14. F	

CHAPTER 3 FILL-IN TEST TOPIC 3A
1. sperm
2. embryo
3. viability
4. fetus
5. German measles
6. intellectual retardation
7. oxygen
8. three
9. Down's Syndrome
10. conception

CHAPTER 3 FILL-IN TEST TOPIC 3B
1. neonate
2. reflexive
3. nervous system
4. visual cliff
5. schema
6. assimilation
7. accommodation
8. conservation
9. formal operations
10. egocentrism
11. Kohlberg
12. collectivist
13. Gilligan
14. Eric Erikson
15. attachment

CHAPTER 3 FILL-IN TEST TOPIC 3C
1. G. Stanley Hall
2. voice
3. puberty
4. menarche
5. identity crisis
6. experimenters
7. secondary sex characteristics
8. five
9. isolation
10. close relationships
11. integration
12. induction
13. stagnation
14. ageism
15. acceptance

CHAPTER 3 MULTIPLE CHOICE TEST TOPIC 3A
1. B	2. A	3. D	4. A	5. C
6. A	7. C	8. D		

CHAPTER 3 MULTIPLE CHOICE TEST TOPIC 3B
1. A	2. D	3. B	4. C	5. D
6. B	7. D	8. C		

CHAPTER 3 MULTIPLE CHOICE TEST TOPIC 3C
1. B	2. D	3. D	4. B	5. C
6. B	7. C	8. A	9. A	10. B
11. A				

CHAPTER 4

CHAPTER 4 MATCHING TOPIC 4A
1. C	2. E	3. B	4. G	5. D
6. H	7. F	8. I	9. A	

CHAPTER 4 MATCHING TOPIC 4B
1. D	2. A	3. K	4. G	5. Q
6. J	7. C	8. H	9. B	10. L
11. E	12. P	13. M	14. R	15. U
16. O	17. N	18. I	19. F	20. S
21. T				

CHAPTER 4 MATCHING TOPIC 4C
1. C	2. I	3. P	4. M	5. A
6. F	7. K	8. D	9. N	10. O
11. B	12. G	13. E	14. J	15. H
16. L				

CHAPTER 4 TRUE-FALSE TEST TOPIC 4A
1. F	2. T	3. F	4. T	5. T
6. T	7. F	8. T	9. F	10. T

CHAPTER 4 TRUE-FALSE TEST TOPIC 4B

1. T   2. T   3. F   4. T   5. F
6. T   7. T   8. T   9. T   10. F
11. F   12. T

CHAPTER 4 TRUE-FALSE TEST TOPIC 4C

1. F   2. T   3. F   4. T   5. F
6. F   7. T   8. T   9. T   10. T
11. T   12. F

CHAPTER 4 FILL-IN TEST TOPIC 4A

1. transducer
2. psychophysics
3. signal detection
4. difference threshold
5. dark adaptation
6. change

CHAPTER 4 FILL-IN TEST TOPIC 4B

1. light
2. purity
3. saturated
4. white light
5. emotion
6. retina
7. cones
8. green
9. opponent-process
10. Ewald Hering

CHAPTER 4 FILL-IN TEST TOPIC 4C

1. amplitude
2. decibel
3. white noise
4. eardrum
5. cochlea
6. taste
7. smell
8. pheromones
9. pressure
10. vestibular
11. pain
12. endorphins

CHAPTER 4 MULTIPLE CHOICE TEST TOPIC 4A

1. C   2. D   3. A   4. C   5. C
6. A   7. B   8. D   9. B   10. D

CHAPTER 4 MULTIPLE CHOICE TEST TOPIC 4B

1. D   2. B   3. A   4. A   5. D
6. C   7. A   8. C   9. A   10. B
11. B   12. D

CHAPTER 4 MULTIPLE CHOICE TEST TOPIC 4C

1. D	2. B	3. A	4. C	5. A
6. D	7. B	8. C	9. B	10. D

CHAPTER 5

CHAPTER 5 MATCHING 5A

1. D	2. E	3. K	4. I	5. M
6. P	7. A	8. G	9. N	10. O
11. Q	12. J	13. B	14. H	15. L
16. C	17. F			

CHAPTER 5 MATCHING 5B

1. I	2. F	3. G	4. A	5. H
6. D	7. B	8. J	9. C	10. K
11. E				

CHAPTER 5 TRUE-FALSE TEST TOPIC 5A

1. T	2. T	3. T	4. F	5. F
6. F	7. T	8. T	9. F	10. T
11. F	12. T			

CHAPTER 5 TRUE-FALSE TEST TOPIC 5B

1. F	2. F	3. T	4. T	5. T
6. T	7. T	8. T	9. F	10. F
11. T	12. F	13. T	14. F	

CHAPTER 5 FILL-IN TEST TOPIC 5A

1. interpretation
2. contrast
3. repetition
4. Gestalt
5. continuity
6. monocular
7. illusion
8. accommodation
9. environment
10. shape constancy

CHAPTER 5 FILL-IN TEST TOPIC 5B

1. Freud
2. selective
3. unconscious
4. electroencephalograph

5. alpha activity
6. REM
7. Freud
8. atonia
9. insomnia
10. suggestion
11. hallucinogens
12. tolerance
13. psychological
14. caffeine
15. depressants

CHAPTER 5 MULTIPLE CHOICE TEST TOPIC 5A

1. A	2. C	3. D	4. C	5. B
6. A	7. D	8. D	9. C	10. A
11. B	12. B	13. D	14. C	15. B

CHAPTER 5 MULTIPLE CHOICE TEST TOPIC 5B

1. A	2. D	3. A	4. C	5. D
6. A	7. B	8. C	9. C	10. A
11. B	12. D	13. D	14. D	15. B
16. C	17. C	18. A		

CHAPTER 6

CHAPTER 6 MATCHING TOPIC 6A

1. J	2. E	3. D	4. H	5. B
6. F	7. K	8. N	9. A	10. I
11. C	12. M	13. G	14. L	

CHAPTER 6 MATCHING TOPIC 6B, C

1. A	2. R	3. K	4. S	5. M
6. T	7. F	8. J	9. G	10. H
11. C	12. I	13. U	14. D	15. O
16. N	17. L	18. B	19. Q	20. E
21. P				

CHAPTER 6 TRUE-FALSE TEST TOPIC 6A

1. T	2. F	3. T	4. T	5. T
6. F	7. T	8. F	9. F	10. F

CHAPTER 6 TRUE-FALSE TEST TOPIC 6B, C

1. T	2. T	3. F	4. T	5. T
6. T	7. F	8. F	9. T	10. T
11. T	12. F	13. F	14. T	15. F

CHAPTER 6 FILL-IN TEST TOPIC 6A

1. Pavlov
2. orienting reflex
3. acquisition
4. unconditioned
5. bell
6. spontaneous recovery
7. generalization
8. discrimination
9. Watson
10. Rescorla

CHAPTER 6 FILL-IN TEST TOPIC 6B AND 6C

1. Thorndike
2. operant
3. environment
4. culture
5. shaping
6. reinforcers
7. primacy
8. base rate
9. piecework
10. intermittent
11. punishment
12. consistent
13. cognitive
14. Bandura
15. vicarious

CHAPTER 6 MULTIPLE CHOICE TEST TOPIC 6A

1. A	2. C	3. A	4. C	5. D
6. C	7. C	8. B	9. D	10. A

CHAPTER 6 MULTIPLE CHOICE TEST TOPIC 6B AND 6C

1. C	2. D	3. C	4. B	5. A
6. B	7. B	8. D	9. C	10. B
11. A	12. A			

CHAPTER 7

CHAPTER 7 MATCHING TOPIC 7A

1. M	2. F	3. D	4. H	5. E
6. I	7. A	8. J	9. L	10. K
11. C	12. G	13. B		

CHAPTER 7 MATCHING TOPIC 7B

1. J	2. N	3. E	4. S	5. I
6. L	7. D	8. A	9. M	10. B
11. G	12. K	13. F	14. C	

CHAPTER 7 TRUE-FALSE TEST TOPIC 7A

1. T	2. T	3. F	4. T	5. T
6. F	7. T	8. F	9. T	10. T
11. T	12. T	13. T	14. F	15. F

CHAPTER 7 TRUE-FALSE TEST TOPIC 7B

1. T	2. T	3. F	4. T	5. F
6. T	7. T	8. F	9. T	10. T
11. T	12. T	13. T	14. T	15. F

CHAPTER 7 FILL-IN TEST TOPIC 7A

1. memory
2. sensory
3. working
4. maintenance rehearsal
5. George Miller
6. repression
7. Loftus
8. semantic
9. autobiographical
10. Tulving

CHAPTER 7 FILL-IN TEST TOPIC 7B

1. recall
2. recognition
3. relearning
4. procedural
5. encoding specificity
6. flashbulb
7. Bower
8. meaningfulness
9. mnemonic devices
10. narrative chaining
11. schemas
12. overlearning
13. retroactive

CHAPTER 7 MULTIPLE CHOICE TEST TOPIC 7A

1. A	2. D	3. C	4. D	5. A
6. A	7. C	8. C	9. A	10. B

CHAPTER 7 MULTIPLE CHOICE TEST TOPIC 7B

1. C	2. B	3. B	4. D	5. B
6. B	7. A	8. C	9. B	10. B
11. D	12. A			

CHAPTER 8

CHAPTER 8 MATCHING TOPIC 8A, B, C
1. L	2. K	3. P	4. I	5. S
6. T	7. U	8. J	9. H	10. A
11. E	12. G	13. B	14. F	15. W
16. D	17. O	18. M	19. N	20. Q
21. R	22. Y	23. V	24. X	25. C

CHAPTER 8 TRUE-FALSE TEST TOPIC 8A
1. T	2. F	3. T	4. T	5. F
6. F	7. F	8. T	9. F	10. T

CHAPTER 8 TRUE-FALSE TEST TOPIC 8B
1. T	2. T	3. F	4. T	5. T
6. F	7. F	8. T	9. F	10. T

CHAPTER 8 TRUE-FALSE TEST TOPIC 8C
1. T	2. T	3. T	4. F	5. T
6. F	7. F	8. T	9. F	10. T

CHAPTER 8 FILL-IN TEST TOPIC 8A
1. well-defined
2. strategy
3. algorithm
4. barriers
5. divergent
6. preparation
7. illumination

CHAPTER 8 FILL-IN TEST TOPIC 8B
1. psycholinguistics
2. symbol
3. pragmatics
4. babbling
5. holophrastic
6. overregularization
7. Chomsky
8. biological

CHAPTER 8 FILL-IN TEST TOPIC 8C
1. objective
2. reliability
3. validity
4. norms
5. Alfred Binet
6. fluid-analytic
7. WAIS-R
8. Terman
9. developmentally delayed
10. Down's syndrome
11. The Bell Curve
12. Arthur Jensen

CHAPTER 8 MULTIPLE CHOICE TEST TOPIC 8A

1. C	2. C	3. A	4. D	5. B
6. B	7. C	8. D	9. B	10. C

CHAPTER 8 MULTIPLE CHOICE TEST TOPIC 8B

1. C	2. A	3. B	4. A	5. D
6. C	7. A	8. A		

CHAPTER 8 MULTIPLE CHOICE TEST TOPIC 8C

1. A	2. B	3. D	4. A	5. C
6. C	7. B	8. C	9. C	10. D
11. B	12. C			

CHAPTER 9

CHAPTER 9 MATCHING TOPIC 9A, B, C

1. H	2. M	3. A	4. O	5. N
6. B	7. L	8. F	9. P	10. K
11. E	12. C	13. I	14. J	15. D
16. G				

CHAPTER 9 TRUE-FALSE TEST TOPIC 9A

1. F	2. T	3. T	4. F	5. F
6. T	7. F	8. F	9. F	10. T
11. T	12. F	13. T	14. F	15. T
16. T	17. F	18. T		

CHAPTER 9 TRUE-FALSE TEST TOPIC 9B

1. F	2. T	3. T	4. T	5. F
6. F	7. F	8. F	9. T	10. T

CHAPTER 9 FILL-IN TEST TOPIC 9A

1. arousal
2. instincts
3. Hull
4. secondary
5. primary
6. Maslow
7. self actualization
8. incentive
9. set point
10. sensation seekers

11. cognitive dissonance
12. Bulimia
13. Henry Murray
14. fear of success
15. affiliation

CHAPTER 9 FILL-IN TEST TOPIC 9B
1. affect
2. Wundt
3. Lazarus
4. Ortony and Turner
5. sympathetic
6. electrical stimulation
7. Darwin
8. Ekman

CHAPTER 9 MULTIPLE CHOICE TEST TOPIC 9A

1. C	2. C	3. A	4. D	5. C
6. D	7. B	8. A	9. C	10. B
11. D	12. B	13. C	14. B	15. A

CHAPTER 9 MULTIPLE CHOICE TEST TOPIC 9B

1. A	2. D	3. B	4. D	5. C
6. D				

CHAPTER 10

CHAPTER 10 MATCHING TOPIC 10A, B

1. S	2. A	3. Z	4. B	5. E
6. X	7. D	8. K	9. Q	10. P
11. V	12. N	13. C	14. H	15. R
16. U	17. L	18. Y	19. F	20. I
21. G	22. J	23. T	24. M	25. O
26. AA	27. W			

CHAPTER 10 TRUE-FALSE TEST TOPIC 10A

1. T	2. T	3. F	4. T	5. F
6. F	7. T	8. F	9. T	10. T
11. T	12. T	13. F	14. T	15. T
16. T	17. F	18. F	19. F	20. T

CHAPTER 10 TRUE-FALSE TEST TOPIC 10B
1. T   2. T   3. T   4. F   5. T
6. F   7. T   8. F

CHAPTER 10 FILL-IN TEST TOPIC 10A
1. theory   2. Mischel
3. psychoanalysis   4. Eros
5. Thanatos   6. regression
7. denial   8. phallic
9. Carl Jung   10. archetypes
11. Alfred Adler   12. habits
13. Rogers   14. trait
15. common

CHAPTER 10 FILL-IN TEST TOPIC 10B
1. interview   2. role playing
3. multiphasic   4. Cattell
5. projective

CHAPTER 10 MULTIPLE CHOICE TEST TOPIC 10A
1. B   2. C   3. D   4. A   5. D
6. C   7. A   8. D   9. B   10. C
11. A   12. C   13. D   14. B   15. C
16. B   17. B   18. A   19. C   20. C
21. D   22. C   23. A   24. C   25. B
26. D

CHAPTER 10 MULTIPLE CHOICE TEST TOPIC 10B
1. B   2. D   3. B   4. A   5. A
6. C   7. A   8. C   9. B   10. D

CHAPTER 11

CHAPTER 11 MATCHING A, B
1. G   2. D   3. A   4. B   5. E
6. C   7. F   8. I   9. H   10. J

CHAPTER 11 TRUE-FALSE TEST TOPIC 11A
1. T	2. T	3. T	4. F	5. T
6. F	7. F	8. T	9. T	10. T
11. F	12. F	13. F	14. F	15. T

CHAPTER 11 TRUE-FALSE TEST TOPIC 11B
1. T	2. T	3. T	4. F	5. T
6. F	7. T	8. T		

CHAPTER 11 FILL-IN TEST TOPIC 11A, B
1. stressor	2. frustration
3. approach-approach	4. avoidance-avoidance
5. change	6. hassles
7. Holmes	8. cognitive reappraisal
9. anxiety	10. frustration
11. Type A	12. exhaustion
13. multiphasia	14. prevention
15. smoking	16. eighty
17. AIDS	

CHAPTER 11 MULTIPLE CHOICE TEST TOPIC 11A
1. A	2. D	3. C	4. D	5. B
6. D	7. B	8. C	9. B	10. D
11. A	12. A	13. B	14. A	15. B
16. C	17. B	18. C	19. D	20. C

CHAPTER 11 MULTIPLE CHOICE TEST TOPIC 11B
1. B	2. D	3. B	4. A	5. C

CHAPTER 12

CHAPTER 12 MATCHING A, B
1. L	2. D	3. R	4. M	5. B
6. N	7. G	8. C	9. Q	10. S
11. O	12. A	13. K	14. T	15. I
16. H	17. P	18. J	19. F	20. E

CHAPTER 12 MATCHING B

1. E	2. J	3. G	4. L	5. O
6. A	7. H	8. M	9. C	10. Q
11. N	12. I	13. D	14. P	15. R
16. K	17. F	18. B		

CHAPTER 12 TRUE-FALSE TEST TOPIC 12A, B

1. T	2. F	3. F	4. T	5. T
6. T	7. F	8. T	9. F	10. T
11. T	12. T	13. F	14. T	15. T
16. T	17. T	18. F	19. F	20. T
21. T	22. F	23. F	24. T	25. F

CHAPTER 12 FILL-IN TEST TOPIC 12A, B

1. DSM-IV
2. insanity
3. comorbidity
4. fear
5. agoraphobia
6. compulsions
7. PTSD
8. Somatoform
9. hypochondriasis
10. Conversion disorder
11. dissociative fugue
12. Paranoid
13. histrionic
14. Delirium
15. Alzheimer's
16. mood
17. mania
18. bipolar disorder
19. schizophrenia
20. Catatonic
21. process
22. Reactive
23. dopamine
24. paranoid
25. Ritalin

CHAPTER 12 MULTIPLE CHOICE TEST TOPIC 12A, B

1. B	2. B	3. A	4. C	5. D
6. A	7. C	8. D	9. B	10. A
11. C	12. A	13. C	14. C	15. C
16. A	17. B	18. B	19. A	20. C
21. B	22. D	23. C	24. A	25. B

CHAPTER 13

CHAPTER 13 MATCHING A, B

1.	B	2.	D	3.	T	4.	S	5.	K
6.	V	7.	U	8.	K	9.	P	10.	R
11.	J	12.	O	13.	L	14.	H	15.	C
16.	F	17.	E	18.	H	19.	A	20.	N
21.	Q	22.	M						

CHAPTER 13 TRUE-FALSE TEST TOPIC 13A

1.	T	2.	F	3.	T	4.	F	5.	T
6.	T	7.	T	8.	F	9.	T	10.	F
11.	F	12.	T	13.	T	14.	T	15.	F

CHAPTER 13 TRUE-FALSE TEST TOPIC 13B

1.	F	2.	T	3.	F	4.	T	5.	T
6.	F	7.	T	8.	T	9.	F	10.	T
11.	F	12.	T	13.	T	14.	F	15.	F
16.	F	17.	T	18.	T	19.	T	20.	T

CHAPTER 13 FILL-IN TEST TOPIC 13A, B

1. priests
2. London
3. Benjamin Rush
4. clinical psychologist
5. psychiatrist
6. psychoanalyst
7. psychosurgery
8. lobotomy
9. shock treatments
10. twelve
11. psychoactive drugs
12. schizophrenia
13. antidepressant
14. Lithium
15. latent
16. transference
17. countertransference
18. client-centered
19. Behavior
20. contingency management
21. contingency contracting
22. cognitive
23. cognitive restructuring
24. deinstitutionalization
25. group

CHAPTER 13 MULTIPLE CHOICE TEST TOPIC 13A, B

1.	C	2.	D	3.	C	4.	D	5.	C
6.	B	7.	A	8.	C	9.	D	10.	A
11.	C	12.	B	13.	D	14.	C	15.	B
16.	B	17.	C	18.	B	19.	C	20.	D
21.	D	22.	C	23.	A	24.	C	25.	B

CHAPTER 14

CHAPTER 14 MATCHING A, B
1. A	2. I	3. P	4. O	5. F
6. S	7. B	8. G	9. L	10. C
11. K	12. D	13. H	14. T	15. J
16. N	17. T	18. J	19. M	20. R

CHAPTER 14 TRUE-FALSE TEST TOPIC 14A
1. T	2. F	3. T	4. T	5. T
6. T	7. F	8. T	9. F	10. T
11. T	12. T	13. F	14. T	15. F

CHAPTER 14 TRUE-FALSE TEST TOPIC 14B
1. F	2. T	3. T	4. F	5. F
6. T	7. F	8. T	9. T	10. T
11. F	12. T			

CHAPTER 14 FILL-IN TEST TOPIC 14A
1. Social psychology
2. attitude
3. observational learning
4. cognitive dissonance
5. Festinger
6. peripheral
7. internal
8. external
9. fundamental attribution
10. reinforcement
11. attachment
12. reciprocity
13. matching

CHAPTER 14 FILL-IN TEST TOPIC 14B
1. conformity
2. obedience
3. Milgram
4. debriefed
5. apathy
6. notice
7. audience inhibition
8. diffusion of responsibility
9. Latane
10. social loafing
11. social facilitation
12. Zajonc
13. Group polarization

CHAPTER 14 MULTIPLE CHOICE TEST TOPIC 14A
1. A	2. C	3. D	4. D	5. C
6. D	7. A	8. C	9. A	10. B
11. B	12. B	13. C	14. D	15. C

CHAPTER 14 MULTIPLE CHOICE TEST TOPIC 14B

1. C	2. A	3. A	4. C	5. B
6. D	7. B	8. B	9. A	10. A

CHAPTER 15

CHAPTER 15 MATCHING A, B

1. D	2. I	3. F	4. B	5. G
6. L	7. H	8. A	9. E	10. J
11. C	12. K	13. M		

CHAPTER 15 TRUE-FALSE TEST TOPIC 15A

1. T	2. T	3. T	4. F	5. T
6. F	7. T	8. T	9. F	10. T
11. T	12. F	13. F	14. F	15. T

CHAPTER 15 TRUE-FALSE TEST TOPIC 15B

1. T	2. F	3. T	4. T	5. T
6. T	7. T	8. T	9. F	10. T

CHAPTER 15 FILL-IN TEST TOPIC 15A

1. job analysis
2. soft
3. bias
4. situational testing
5. validity
6. Expectancy
7. Adams
8. goal setting
9. job satisfaction
10. age

CHAPTER 15 FILL-IN TEST TOPIC 15B

1. Environmental
2. personal space
3. intimate
4. social
5. territoriality
6. primary
7. population density
8. neurotoxins
9. Sports
10. billiards

CHAPTER 15 MULTIPLE CHOICE TEST TOPIC 15A

1. A	2. B	3. D	4. C	5. B
6. D	7. D	8. A	9. D	10. C
11. A	12. C			

CHAPTER 15 MULTIPLE CHOICE TEST TOPIC 15B

1. D	2. C	3. B	4. D	5. B
6. A	7. C	8. C	9. A	10. B

STATISTICAL APPENDIX

APPENDIX MATCHING

1. L	2. J	3. H	4. I	5. B
6. D	7. A	8. C	9. G	10. E
11. F	12. K			

APPENDIX TRUE-FALSE TEST

1. T	2. F	3. F	4. T	5. T
6. F	7. T	8. T	9. F	10. F

APPENDIX FILL-IN TEST

1. frequency distribution
2. histogram
3. median
4. mean
5. mode
6. standard deviation
7. inferential
8. normal curve
9. statistically significant
10. range

APPENDIX MULTIPLE CHOICE TEST

1. A	2. D	3. D	4. A	5. B
6. B	7. D	8. D	9. C	10. C